Challenging Minds

Challenging Minds

Thinking Skills
and Enrichment Activities

by
Lynne Kelly

Prufrock Press Inc.
P.O. Box 8813
Waco, TX 76714-8813
Phone: (800) 998-2208
Fax: (800) 240-0333
http://www.prufrock.com

Prufrock Press Inc.
P.O. Box 8813
Waco, TX 76714-8813
(800) 998-2208
http://www.prufrock.com

Dedication

For Rebecca, James, and Cameron—who demanded enrichment.

Acknowledgments

I would like to acknowledge the invaluable assistance of LeoNora Cohen in reading the manuscript and making extensive suggestions, especially in the area of metacognosis.

I would also like to acknowledge the enthusiastic input from the Challenge Studies students of Ballarat and Queens Anglican Grammar in Australia while testing this course over five years.

Without the continual support of Damian Kelly, in discussing every challenge and proofreading the material at every stage, there would have been no book.

Contents

Foreword

Foreword

How would your life be different if, on your first day of class of the new school year, your students became so excited and thoughtful about the tasks you set that they asked for more? And how would your life be different if you found curricular materials that were filled with mind-stretching activities, were interdisciplinary, empowered students, encouraged independence, and did this with good-humored grace? Lynne Kelly's book, *Challenging Minds: Enrichment for Able Adolescents,* is the type of material that can really make your classroom different in these positive ways.

Challenging Minds is a thought-provoking, intriguing, and tantalizing collection of mind-stretching challenges for able adolescents. Each of the 14 activities, usually completed over a period of a few weeks, provokes the highest levels of thinking in Bloom's Taxonomy: analysis, synthesis, and/or evaluation. An unusual and excellent feature of these materials is the emphasis on metacognition (awareness of one's own thinking). By reflecting on their processing and the success or failure of their strategies, students are empowered to become better thinkers. Rather than focusing on what to learn, the emphasis is on *how* to learn, helping students develop the tools needed to function successfully in the information age. These activities teach students how to think, regardless of the subject matter.

Such a collection of enrichment activities for able secondary students is a rare and welcome addition to the field of gifted education. All too often, gifted students in secondary schools are simply accelerated. Although acceleration is a useful option for many gifted students, unless the accelerated curriculum is differentiated by explicit focus on open-endedness, abstractness, complexity, critical and creative thinking, and metacognition (all aspects of *Challenging Minds*), students are simply asked to remember facts faster.

One of the features that makes this book outstanding is that each activity has been field-tested for at least five years in secondary classrooms. The reactions of students, and the possible pitfalls the teacher may encounter, are clearly and often humorously elucidated. You know this material has been used successfully with students.

ix

Challenging Minds

Challenging Minds was written to stimulate higher-level thinking and metacognition in gifted students. The introductory section provides background information that ensures confidence for the novice and offers justification for the use of these materials to teachers well-versed in teaching thinking strategies. The rationale discusses the learning patterns of able adolescents, including their curiosity, use of humor, sense of relationships, creativity, logical thinking, and heightened moral and emotional development. How-to's and classroom applications deal with the amount of time for the challenges, how to get started, the importance of student self-evaluation, assessment of how challenges have been used in schools, and the role of the teacher. A discussion of Bloom's Taxonomy upon which the thinking activities are based is followed by a section on metacognition, or "thinking about thinking." This metacognitive aspect helps students become aware of the processes they have selected and asks them to consider how successful they were in attaining their goals. The section concludes with an annotated overview of each of the 14 challenges related to the metacognitive features. The remainder of the book details each of the challenges that range from a deceptively straightforward finding of answers to a range of knowledge and comprehension questions in the first challenge (but the complexity is in analyzing how one goes about the process efficiently and effectively!), to activities on such diverse topics as cryogenics, advertising, starting a restaurant, or paradoxes.

Kelly uses the challenges in three ways, depending on both the nature of the challenge and the nature of the student. First, activities are used with special classes of identified gifted students. Second, challenges are offered to small, informal groups of self-selected students. And finally, they are used with individuals as spare-time activities to keep them interested after they have finished regular classwork for other teachers. However, I believe that even though the challenges are intended as enrichment activities for the gifted, many, if not most, of the activities could be used in the regular classroom with other students!

One difficulty with providing enrichment activities for some secondary gifted students is motivating them to invest time and effort if their work is not recognized for assessment. By incorporating these challenges in the regular classroom and by having students *self-assess on criteria provided for each activity* students are recognized for the importance of their efforts. They also are empowered to judge their own work. If they have already earned an A their grade could go to an A+. On the other hand, many able students are so bored with school subjects, they would be grateful for this type of stimulating curriculum and would need no external rewards. Compacting the regular curriculum by assessing students who want to complete required material early would provide time to do challenges. The opportunity to share their efforts might also be a reward. If the teacher recognizes a strong student interest, a challenge could be modified to better relate to that interest, which is usually highly motivating. With able students, mandatory use of challenges should be avoided. Once some students get started and begin to laugh and enjoy the activities, others will surely follow.

If used in the regular classroom, certainly not all students will be able to complete all activities at the same level. What will differ is the rate at which they learn (not necessarily the speed they find answers); the terminal level or end point (the more able students will reach higher levels); the number of repetitions needed for permanent memory; ease of information retrieval; the ability to generalize, abstract, and see relationships; and the learning trajectory, which will be much steeper for brighter students (Cohen, 1990). You may find, for example, that the whole class could do the first part of #7 Laughable Logic—perhaps in a personal development class to deal with what humor is appropriate for school—but only the able learners or those who really want to go on would tackle the more complex classifying aspect of this activity. However, all students can and will make progress in becoming better thinkers. All students can benefit from these mind-stretching activities and some seemingly average students may even demonstrate unseen abilities when given challenges.

In fact, *Challenging Minds* fits with several of the principles central to education of gifted students that should belong to all. These can be summarized as Six Simple Rules (Cohen, 1991, 1992):

1. *Focus on the unique pattern of strengths: the abilities, competencies, and talents of each individual child.*
   Through some of these activities, students not normally seen as gifted may find that their abilities in visual, practical, social, or other domains allow them to perform very successfully on challenges. Both teachers and students may identify strengths not normally apparent in regular classwork.

2. *Group students by interests or abilities at least part of the time in order to enhance social and emotional development.*
   Students can be grouped by interest or ability to work on these activities. Not all students have to do all challenges, and they may

group themselves or be assigned to groups. Some activities are especially conducive to group work and most challenges should be processed with others upon completion.

3. *Encourage students to move as far and as fast in the basic skills as possible—offer flexible pacing.*
   With the exception of the first challenge, students can work at their own pace to complete activities.

4. *Enrich individual interests. Provide opportunities to explore, in depth, areas in which students are greatly interested.*
   Students have the opportunity to explore interests in realistic situations. The challenges offer multiple "jumping off points" for students to become engaged in problems that are real to them and to pursue them in-depth for as long as they wish.

5. *Provide the tools for life-long learning (Cohen, 1987):*

   • *Research skills—for accessing information;*

   • *Higher order thinking skills—for processing information;*

   • *Creativity skills for modifying, adapting, or transforming information;*

   • *Communication skills—for sharing information and ideas;*

   • *Study skills—for organization and time management; and*

   • *Metacognition—for empowerment through self-regulation and control of learning.*

The heart of *Challenging Minds* is the emphasis on these life-long learning skills.

6. *Offer mediation, counseling, guidance, and facilitation from caring adults to optimize potential (see Betts, 1985; Clark, 1988; Gallagher, 1985; Kaplan, 1974; Maker, 1982; Renzulli & Reis, 1985; Van Tassel-Baska, 1988; Ward, 1980).*
   These challenges need you, the caring teacher, to make them work. Your enthusiasm is needed to stimulate interest in tackling the task. Your willingness to make the classroom safe so students can explore and learn from mistakes is also important. Reassurance that they may use a variety of paths to get to the end point, and that cre-

ativity, especially in certain challenges, is desirable and essential. Your facilitation but not direct giving of answers is needed. Your own curiosity, puzzlement, and reflective thinking provides a role model students need for becoming thinking, reflective young people. Your enjoyment of the humorous aspects of the challenges will encourage laughter and avoid paralyzing perfectionism. And finally, your recognition of their abilities and support through their struggles to think will help students reach their goals.

But how to include these challenges in the regular classroom? Kelly suggests that the focus is interdisciplinary, as they do not easily fit into one subject area. On the other hand, once you read through a couple of the challenges, you will likely see connections to at least some of the topics that you are teaching. For example, if you are an English teacher, starting your class with the first activity that focuses on how to go about finding answers to lots of different types of questions would be a natural for your teaching of research skills. The bonus is that the activity is much like a *people search* and helps students begin to work with and learn from each other. Other challenges that might be particularly suitable to the English classroom could be #2, Debates, Arguments and All-out Brawls, which is related to seeing various points of view; #4, Blinding Blurb, in which the student considers the nature of language; #7 which focuses on humor; #8 which focuses on interpretation; and #14 which looks at paradoxes. Because each of these challenges is interdisciplinary, they could also be used in other subject areas.

If you are a science teacher, naturals for your classes are #9, Photocopying Mirrors, which has even provoked some heated discussions among physics professors; #3, Show Me You, which deals with the magnitude of such huge and minute scales as the universe and atomic particles and their relationship to self-concept; or #12, The Future is Cool, which gets into the science (and plenty of other areas with great fun) of cryonics. If you teach social studies, naturals to incorporate into your classroom are #6, Here Worship, when you are discussing leadership; #8, A.A. Milne—Poet or Psychic?, in which the interpretation of material relates to how an anthropologist or historian might try to make sense of a document (yes, it also fits with English); or #11, Problematic Probing, which could be used to learn about investigating belief systems. Other challenges are suitable for math (#5, #11, or #13). Yet these are only starting points.

A challenge to classroom teachers is to see which activities are appropriate and how to use them, because they will help you change your views of the teaching-learning process. A creative, thoughtful teacher can easily incorporate at least several of the activities into almost any subject area and can justify his or her inclusion because of his or her value for life-long learning. After all, *all* teachers are supposed to be teaching thinking. I took the liberty of sharing the draft of *Challenging Minds* with several teachers from different secondary disciplines and even from the primary level. Their unanimous and enthusiastic response was: "How soon can I get the book to use in my classroom?"

—LeoNora Cohen, Ph.D.

Introduction

Three common approaches are used for students perceived to have high intellectual potential. These are acceleration, extension, and enrichment. All are of great value. This book is designed to be used as an enrichment course, exposing such students to activities which would not be experienced in the usual subject-based curriculum. The tasks are cross-curricular and could not be classified as extension in any accepted subject area. They are also context based, in that most allow students to follow realistic interests in realistic situations. The emphasis can be adjusted to match the particular talents of the students involved in the course.

Challenging Minds consists of 14 challenges which vary in complexity. Each challenge poses a problem and asks students to formulate a response. All tasks are open in nature and permit a variety of approaches as well as a variety of final reports.

For each challenge, there is a guideline to tackling the challenge, and a set of teacher notes. From challenge 2 on, there is a component asking students to consider their own thought processes. This section is headed "Thinking about Thinking."

Each task takes the form of a challenge designed to develop the student's skills in a number of areas simultaneously. These challenges are not intended to be completed in a single sitting, such as a school period. The tasks have been designed to take the students into the higher levels of Bloom's Taxonomy of cognitive behavior which emphasize the skills of evaluation, synthesis, and analysis. The lower levels of knowledge, comprehension, and application are obviously also appropriate; however, the emphasis is on the higher level and more abstract skills. Particular applications to Bloom's levels are given in the teachers' notes for each challenge.

Intellectually gifted children are differentiated in a number of ways. These vary, depending on which reference you read, but there are a number of characteristics which are common to all references—and it is these I have concentrated on when designing the challenges.

Gifted students are known to have a higher sense of self-awareness and sensitivity to feelings. They tend to possess high expectations of themselves and may resist attempting a task in a way which will cause lower results. The challenges are designed to avoid such tick/cross assessment, encouraging students to take risks. In preference to only marking the final product, I have used the students' own analysis of their methods to evaluate their work; therefore, "making mistakes" and taking risks will not cause lower assessments.

Gifted children are often identified early due to their incessant questioning of their world. They exhibit a great curiosity. This trait has been addressed particularly in challenges 1, 3, 4, 5, 6, 9, and 12.

Gifted children are also noted for their keen sense of humor. Often they are perceived as laughing at different things from other students. I have tried to allow this to play a large part in the challenges (particularly challenges 4, 7, 8, and 12).

The ability to see relationships and patterns in situations is often noted with gifted students. This ability has been targeted in a number of the challenges. These children are known to identify such relationships earlier and more clearly than their age peers (particularly challenges 3, 7, 10, 11, and 12).

Imagination, initiative, creativity, and an individualistic approach to tackling tasks are traits which have been associated with giftedness. Most of the challenges have been designed to incorporate these within the scope of the response required. I have found the need to vary the actual challenge definitions, when applicable, to enhance the opportunity for a student to follow a different approach (particularly challenges 3, 5, 6, 7, 8, and 12).

The invaluable skill of clear, logical thinking is targeted in challenges 2, 4, 9, 13, and 14.

Many references quote a heightened moral, emotional, and philosophical development with gifted students. A number of the challenges have been designed to incorporate such aspects (particularly challenges 2, 3, 6, 10, 11, and 12).

Many of the tasks are much better attempted over a number of weeks to allow students to mull over the approaches they are to use. It is an aim of all challenges to encourage the students to broaden their definitions of "resource" and "method" and to optimize their skills in using both. They are also characterized by the ability to work for greater lengths of time and at greater depths than their age peers. All the challenges are to be done over a reasonable span of time. During the course, I have interspersed the challenges with shorter tasks of the more common puzzle or single-activity format.

I have often started courses with the first challenge presented in this book. This is a far more structured challenge than the rest, and one which does have a more defined solution. The questions are carefully selected to help students broaden the two terms defined above.

Evaluation of the method by which they completed the challenge, and a realistic but constructive self-criticism of their final product, is to be highly recommended if they are to gain maximum benefit from attempting the tasks.

To assist teachers who wish to assess the responses to the challenges, a set of criteria has been proposed. The responses to the challenges can vary greatly and students may negotiate a change in the way they respond to the challenge. Consequently, the work produced may deviate from the expected form and teachers may need to adjust the assessment criteria as they see fit. Gifted students should be permitted to use their creativity, but this may require teachers to use the suggested criteria equally creatively!

In using the criteria, teachers may wish to give a grade for each and then average the grades for an overall rating. If the teacher feels one criterion is more important than the others, she or he may wish to weight the grading for each giving more value to certain criteria, and hence construct a final grade.

I have usually graded the response to the challenge and the "Thinking about Thinking" section separately. This has been important when a student has performed very poorly on the challenge and then analyzed the reason very well. This has been the case for a number of under-achieving gifted students whose motivation or self-concept has been cause for concern. This separation allowed these two aspects to be clearly differentiated and valuable discussion and counseling has arisen from the "Thinking about Thinking" responses. For reasons of school assessment requirements, these two grades were then combined.

Enjoy the challenge!

—Lynne Kelly

Classroom Applications of the Challenges

I have used the challenge assignments in three ways.

First, I have used many of them with groups in a timed class. Some, such as "The Future is Cool," are more valuable in this situation. There are examples of students whose performance at school has not been outstanding but who have revealed unrecognized talents when tackling the challenges.

Second, I have used them with smaller, self-selecting, informal groups. The "Photocopying Mirrors" challenge has been extremely successful in this case. I have heard arguments relating to this assignment months after the initial students began it.

Third, I have used these challenges with individuals. Some students are bored with classes in which they complete the work quickly and easily. Some teachers are too busy, with good reason, to extend work in a stimulating way. Most of these assignments require little equipment other than books and time. Students can take the assignments to class and continue with such work when they have completed their classwork to the classroom teacher's satisfaction. They can also work on them in their spare time.

Methodology

It is essential to stimulate enthusiasm for tackling the challenge. If the pathway to completing the task is obvious, as it is with most linear tasks set in schools, there is little point in doing it to develop the skills involved in designing a methodology and tackling a task which has no correct solution. This is the nature of most tasks to be faced in future life.

Students used to linear tasks will initially respond with concern as to their ability to "complete" the challenges. I have to emphasize that it is the very actions of attempting and making wrong moves which is part of the learning. I have endeavored to use some starting point which will catch the attention of our more talented students. In most cases, these students have a greater sense of the ridiculous—and I have tried to use this quality. Sometimes I have used humor to attract their attention, such as in "A. A. Milne—Poet or Psychic?" and sometimes included tasks within the challenge which allow them to exhibit their own humor, such as in the advertising section of "The Future is Cool."

In all challenges, the aim is to gain cognitive skills more than create the product requested by the assignment. It is essential that students are made aware of the aims of this course and are encouraged to discover the joys of using their abilities.

Bloom's Taxonomy

Benjamin Bloom, in 1956, chaired a committee which published the *Taxonomy of Educational Objectives, Cognitive Domain* which sought to clarify and define the various levels of cognitive functioning. This would allow a form of classification of the intellectual demands made by various assessment procedures or teaching objectives. This taxonomy is now widely used as a system for conceptualizing the various levels of thinking required to complete a given task.

It is this taxonomy which will be used throughout this text to assess the cognitive skills which are being addressed by each challenge.

The taxonomy consists of six levels:

1. **Knowledge**
   This level is the most common level in standard curricular activities. It consists of activities which relate to the transmission and acquisition of information.

   > For example: The student will be able to provide the correct answers to questions such as: Who wrote *The Hitchhiker's Guide to the Galaxy*?

   The student's role at this level is passive.

2. **Comprehension**
   This level focuses on understanding new information presented. There is a need to find meaning in the information learned or stud-

ied. This involves a more interactive role for the student involved in the challenge.

> For example: Explain why Ford Prefect wanted to convince the Vogon guard to reconsider his career options in *The Hitchhiker's Guide to the Galaxy.*

3. **Application**
   This level involves using methods, concepts, principles, and theories, and applying them to new situations in a concrete way. The teacher's role becomes less dominant while the student must take a more active role.

   > For example: Given the rules of mathematics, solve the following real problem: A farmer has ...

   > Write a poem which fits the accepted definitions of a ballad.

4. **Analysis**
   Analyzing a problem or situation involves breaking down the information into its constituent elements and explaining the relationships between them. The process can involve the identification of patterns, clarification of the underlying structure, determining the foundation principles, and gaining a fuller understanding of the context.

   The student has to do most of the work, under the guidance of the teacher.

   > For example: Why are some graphs continuous while others have discontinuities?

   > There are a number of forms of holding data (memory and storage) in computers. When a program is run which calculates the square of a number, what forms of memory/storage are being used?

5. **Synthesis**
   This process is a creative one. In synthesizing a solution, the student must take the constituent elements and fit them together in such a way as to create a whole which serves as a solution to the problem.

They must integrate ideas and information, theories, and methods within the limits of the environment of the problem.

The student is now required to incorporate creative thinking with all the other levels below it. Consequently, this level must be heavily based on the student's individual work.

For example: Write a letter to a politician, arguing your opinion on a crucial current issue.

Develop a hypothesis on why some people have almost obsessive favorites when it comes to reading matter.

6. **Evaluation**

The highest level of cognitive skill, according to Bloom, is evaluation. This level involves the judging of ideas and solutions according to a set of criteria. In making judgments, students must establish criteria and apply them in decision making. The lower levels are obviously involved when working at this level, but students are using their own skills under the encouragement of the teacher.

For example: Develop a set of guidelines by which to judge modern literature. According to your guidelines, rate the novels available in order of merit and justify your claims.

(Please note: the above example could be simply done at the knowledge level: *The Hitchhiker's Guide to the Galaxy*—one and only!)

Thinking about Thinking (Metacognosis)

There is ample evidence to show the benefits of analyzing not only the product resulting from the project, but also the methodology. Metacognitive processes, or thinking about the thinking process, is becoming a very popular educational theme. In the challenges, a metacognitive component, under the "Thinking about Thinking" heading has been included. Time is rarely given to such activities in the normal classroom. By becoming more conscious of these processes it is believed students can greatly enhance their performance in a range of creative and productive activities. It is hoped such learning will be applied to all aspects of the student's academic pursuits.

In some cases, the benefits are far more wide reaching. Students' analyses of their thought processes, monitored during the activities associated with the challenge "Debates, Arguments, and All-out Brawls," have led to a consideration of the optimum environment for logical thought. Some students found the shower a great place, others the quiet at their desks. Many were able to identify marked differences in their degree of logical thinking in emotive situations—for example, in the middle of a debate about which they had strong personal feelings. Some found situations in which they just couldn't see the other side of the argument due to their personal situation. Being conscious of these influences can only be of benefit to them in both the academic and non-academic aspects of their lives.

Examining the Challenges

The various challenges are enrichment activities in their own rights. A further dimension can be gained from the course by monitoring the thinking involved and analyzing what has gone on. The challenges allow different aspects of the metacognitive process to be explored. In doing so, valuable comparisons can be made between what has been discovered in each of the challenges.

The challenges may be considered, for such a comparison, in the following way:

1. "Get the Answers"
   An introductory challenge which is more straightforward than the rest. It allows the concepts of methodology and metacognosis to be introduced.

2. "Debates, Arguments, and All-out Brawls"
   This challenge involves logical thought. Metacognitive analysis involves the effect of various influences, emotional and physical, on logical thinking.

3. "Show Me You (and the universe and an atom)"
   Creativity in presentation and response to self-concept is the basis of this challenge. Monitoring such processes should contrast sharply with those considered in challenge 2.

4. "Blinding Blurb"
   Ideally, jargon task with which students are familiar and unfamiliar will be encountered in areas in this. Preliminary judgments can vary based on this factor alone. There is also a need to approach companies to find out the meaning of their advertisements. The apprehension at doing this, for some students, will impede their ability to proceed.

5. "Nourish and Flourish"
   Decision making is often based on priorities, some of which we may apply unconsciously. This challenge includes analyzing the student's application of priorities to restaurant design.

6. "Hero Worship (or: Elvis Presley is better than Albert Einstein)"
   The effect of hero status on our ability to judge the words and actions of a "hero" is investigated. This challenge leads on to thinking about the thought processes of followers and their leaders.

7. "Laughable Logic"
   This challenge can be used to explore the effects of distraction, inflexibility, and response to criticism on achieving a goal. The task includes monitoring thinking in situations which allow these aspects to be explored.

8. "A. A. Milne—Poet or Psychic?"
   How much do people's beliefs affect their thinking about new ideas? The level of concentration and effect of humor on thinking are also explored in this challenge. The influence of suspicion and gullibility on thought processes are also raised.

9. "Photocopying Mirrors"
   This is a straightforward problem-solving exercise with some diversions along the way. It is used to analyze the thinking and methodology involved when given a solvable problem to pursue. The actual solution is such that a number of propositions are possible which can lead to valid arguments similar to that in many scientific investigations.

10. "Dare to be Different: A Hypothesis"
    In this case, the "Thinking about Thinking" section is not included in the actual task description. The aim is to look back and recognize whether the objective was to accept or reject a hypothesis. The

research is subsequently done with that aim in mind. Ideally, students investigate the situation and then examine the hypothesis. (Maybe some combination would be the optimum.) This is the discussion theme to follow the completion of the task.

11. "Problematic Probing"
   The emotional content of the task can greatly affect the way in which it is handled. This challenge includes the contrasts of trying to find out what people believe about God and analyzing the results statistically. By keeping a journal throughout the process, the effect of the need for sensitivity and the emotional content can be analyzed.

12. "The Future is Cool (for Kold Korp.)"
   This is a long and very popular challenge which allows application of the findings of the previous "Thinking about Thinking" sections. The assignment takes a number of weeks and is variable enough to allow regular review of progress in terms of metacognitive skills. A number of questions are included to be addressed throughout the task.

Single-task Thinking

The last two challenges have been specifically designed to examine the deepest level of concentration with which a student can cope. I call this level of concentration "Single-task Thinking." An explanatory note is given before challenge 13.

13. "If Fred's Hat is Purple, What Is the Name of Mary's Dog?"
   This challenge uses a standard puzzle format to examine concentration levels. Puzzles are completed and designed to allow many examples during which to monitor concentration levels.

14. "Please Ignore This Heading"
   Using 40 paradoxes, the levels of concentration are further analyzed. The paradoxes vary greatly in difficulty. In many, the problem is explaining the logical conclusions from accepting the statement. Students can be made to concentrate to "exhaustion" quite quickly when required to explain paradoxes.

Challenging Minds

This collection of challenges allows students to become familiar with a large range of metacognitive processes. Hopefully, they will use this knowledge to optimize the application of their thinking skills in all aspects of life.

The Challenges

Challenge 1
Get the Answers

This challenge requires you to find the answers to the following 100 questions. You may use *any* resource you like, except other students in the class. Each student is to work independently.

The Aim

1. To broaden the concept of "resources" to include a greater variety of references and recognize the value of other people's abilities and knowledge.

2. To gain experience seeking out information in a variety of ways.

3. To improve efficiency in tackling a sizable task.

4. To develop skills in evaluating personal methodology.

Method

1. Write a brief report on the following and submit it for review at the end of the assignment:
   a. What is your definition of a "resource"?
   b. Describe briefly how you will go about tackling the task of finding the answers.
   c. How do you think you will approach the task in order to gain as many answers as possible within the time limit?

2. Within the given time limit, gain as many of the answers as possible. With each answer, record the source of the response.

3. Having corrected the answers and re-read your initial comments, write a report on what you have learned, including responses to the following:
   a. Has your definition of a "resource" changed in any way?
      Do all resources have the same reliability? If not, does this affect their usefulness? Are there examples of when a less reliable source is still of great value?
   b. Given the task again would you approach it differently? If so, how and why?

• •

c. Did the way you actually recorded the responses affect your efficiency? If so, how?

d. Were there any aspects of your method which were particularly good and could be recommended to others?

e. Are there any steps you would include in tackling another sizable task which you would now consider valuable?

Questions

1. What is the German word for "horse"?
2. What is the Queen of England's family name?
3. How is e-knee-bree-ated (drunk out of your mind) spelled?
4. Who was the king of the gods in Greek mythology?
5. Who wrote *Pride and Prejudice*?
6. When did Albert Einstein win the Nobel Prize?
7. Would you serve Amanita phalloides for dinner if you liked the guest?
8. What is the most recent figure you can get for the population of Botswana?
9. What is the telephone number for the Federal Patent Office?
10. How do you calculate the gear ratio on a bicycle?
11. What is El Reno, OK's zipcode?
12. What were the names of the two families in the War of the Roses?
13. Why is LaBrea, CA, famous?
14. Who played Velvet in the original version of *National Velvet*?
15. How far is it from Moscow to Paris by air (if you ignored little details like flight paths and flew directly between the cities)?
16. What is the capital of Botswana?
17. What is the Apgar test?
18. In what sport is the pommelhorse used?
19. What does the S R (followed by a number) mean on the side of tires?
20. What are the ingredients for a white sauce?
21. What is the other instrument usually played by the musician who plays a Cor Anglais in an orchestra?
22. What does the electronics term LED stand for?
23. What is the second last letter of the Greek alphabet?
24. What is the area of Lake Michigan?
25. Who won the first Nobel Peace Prize?
26. Of what did Marie Curie die?
27. Who wrote *The Hobbit*?
28. Who was president of the United States in 1939?
29. What is the new name for Upper Volta?
30. What does the term "caveat emptor" mean?

31. What year did the Titanic sink?
32. When was the Murrah Federal Building in Oklahoma bombed?
33. Who is the weekday news anchor for the ABC evening news?
34. What is the name of the publisher of *The Wall Street Journal*?
35. What is the lowest temperature, in degrees Celsius, which is theoretically possible?
36. What planet is closest in size to the Earth?
37. What is the number of calories in a 1 pound potato?
38. What is the Dewey number for The Bible?
39. What do the letters LLP stand for in the legal profession?
40. Why is a Catholic who has S. J. after his name respected?
41. Who are the senators from in your state?
42. What does the musical term 'sul ponticello' mean?
43. If your power went off, what is the phone number to call?
44. Who wrote *Crime and Punishment*?
45. Who played Rhett Butler in "Gone with the Wind"?
46. What percentage of the Australian population is literate?
47. Who wrote *Northanger Abbey*?
48. In what field of endeavor did Piaget make his mark?
49. What is the population density of Hong Kong?
50. What is the name of the eldest sister in *Pride and Prejudice*?
51. What is the current Olympic record for men's shot put?
52. What zip codes do you put on a letter to Greenville, TX?
53. What was an "alchemist"?
54. What is the full name of the author of *The Hobbit*?
55. Name the events in the modern pentathlon.
56. What is a papillon when it is not a film or the French word for butterfly?
57. What is the telephone number of the nearest international airport?
58. How old is the president of the United States of America?
59. Who won the War of the Roses?
60. What do S4 and S2 mean to a pharmacist?
61. How many lifeboats were on the Titanic?
62. How many people died in the Murrah Federal Building bombing?
63. What is the average height of a papillon?
64. What is an Allen key?
65. What is the address of the ABC television stations in your state?
66. What is the eleventh letter of the Greek alphabet?
67. What island in Lake Michigan bears the name of a city which is a long way away, and a state which is even further?

68. Who is the publisher of *Hitchhiker's Guide to the Galaxy*?

69. Is the oboe a single-reed or double-reed instrument?

70. Who prints *The New York Times*?

71. What was Fyodor Dostoevsky's first published novel?

72. In what card game is the Goren point count method of contract bidding used?

73. What is the ISBN prefix for Berkeley Publishers?

74. What is one *dram*?

75. What is a Vombatus ursinus?

76. To what court do you go to be tried for murder?

77. What is the percentage literacy of the population of Chad for men and separately, for women?

78. What is the German word for "please"?

79. What is the meaning of the word which is pronounced ewe-bick-quit-us?

80. What is the Leakey family famous for?

81. What is the other clef which has the same symbol as the tenor clef but is in a different position on the staff?

82. Who was claimed to be the wife of Zeus in Greek mythology?

83. Would you feed Agaricus arvensis to a guest of whom you were particularly fond?

84. Who is the tallest recorded person, living or dead? How tall was this person?

85. What does "NIDA" stand for?

86. Who was Charles I's father?

87. What is the German word for "bread"?

88. Why can't most people grow an Avicennia marina in their backyard?

89. What is the longest recorded distance for Haggis Hurling?

90. How many inches are there in a furlong?

91. What is a "musette" in musical jargon?

92. Who was Marie Curie's husband?

93. For what topic did Albert Einstein win the Nobel Prize for Physics?

94. What is the fertility rate (births per childbearing woman) in Benin? (This is the average! Try comparing it to some more familiar countries.)

95. What is the speed of sound in air?

96. Which title of a book by Dostoevsky is a description of himself when he fell victim to an addictive activity?

97. Who was the priestess of Hera at Argos who was loved by Zeus? He gave her the shape of a heifer to conceal her from his wife.

98. What is the scientific name for the hairy-nosed wombat?

99. Who was the mother of Charles II of England?

100. How many seconds in a fortnight?

Teacher's Notes

Bloom's Taxonomy

This task introduces students to the cognitive level of evaluation, the highest in the taxonomy. In all challenges there is enormous benefit in evaluating the method by which they approached and worked through the task. By using a fairly straightforward challenge initially, this skill can be developed for use in all future assignments. There is an obvious amount of knowledge involved in these challenges.

Cognitive Level

This activity focuses on interest in information. Bright students also enjoy the challenge of gaining information.

By giving them skills in identifying the source of a range of information, and methods to gain it efficiently, they can visualize their knowledge base like the back-up storage for a computer. They don't need it all in their heads, as long as it is readily available.

Personal Characteristics

The aim is also to give them a working familiarity with other sources of information such as year books, unusual specialist texts, and government departments. The natural curiosity of gifted students makes these resources a source of pleasure as well as information.

The major effort-saving device available is to plan the use of resources—especially that crucial resource called time. There are many later questions which will require exactly the same resource (e.g. three questions require words from a German dictionary). Most students will not plan their approach initially. They will soon realize the benefit of doing so. There is no need to warn them of this. They will learn!

General Notes

Students have used various techniques successfully. Usually they rush in, waste some time, and need a few revisits before they conclude that a planning session will ultimately save a great deal of time. Successful methods have included color coding the questions or listing the numbers of questions which will be found in the same reference or location. Some have also retained a list of questions under the heading "haven't got the foggiest," and keep asking until someone enlightens them.

It is also interesting to note that scribbling answers all over the worksheet creates problems in optimizing the use of time. Discussing different research methods as a group is important.

Encourage students to recognize the value of people as a resource. Several difficult questions have been included to motivate students to ask other people for assistance. If they don't know how to approach a question, someone will know the answers, or, if not, at least they will know where to find it.

A student once confessed to "cheating" because she received help from her mother. I had a great deal of difficulty convincing her that mothers were not only mothers but valid resources as well! Many students are quite amazed by how much their parents know.

The easiest way to generate a new set of questions, should you wish to use the challenge with another group, is to ask 20 people for two questions each. The useful ones, along with your own, will give you 30 to 40 different themes. By going to the appropriate sources you will soon find other related questions to construct a set such as the one provided.

At the end of this challenge, students should appreciate the concepts of using a broad range of resources as well as optimizing their use of time. They will also develop the ability to monitor their own thinking, methodology, and success. From this monitoring it is hoped students will improve their cognitive processes.

The foundations for development in these areas have been laid. The awareness of personal (affective) processes, as now recognized, should be referred to in future challenges for development.

Assessment

Criteria
To what level did the student:
1. get the answers correct?
2. identify the source of information for each answer?
3. produce a broad-ranging definition of resources?
4. discuss the use of resources addressing reliability, usefulness, and relevance of each type?
5. discuss the effect of methodology, such as the collection of resources, on efficiency?
6. discuss the ways in which such a methodology could be improved, being both constructive in criticism and realistic in strategies?

Answer	Suggested sources	Comment
1. das pferd	German dictionary	If they put the dictionary away now they will regret not reading ahead to number 78 and 87.
2. Windsor	older family members encyclopedia, history text	
3. inebriated	dictionary	
4. Zeus	classical dictionary encyclopedia informed person	
5. Jane Austen	librarian parents literature text	Many people will know the answer— even an English teacher
6. 1921	encyclopedia	This is a case where people will not usually be reliable.
7. No, it is highly toxic	botanical reference encyclopedia use of specialist	This is the first of a number of questions designed to introduce the classification texts. This plant is very deadly!
8. 205,300 (1988)	Britannica Year Book	Many students will discover this book and forget the questions! It often fascinates them.
9. (703) 557-4636	telephone book directory assistance	Learning to fathom the government section of the telephone book is a challenge in itself.
10. Divide the number of teeth on chain wheel by number of teeth on free wheel	bike enthusiast specialist text	The answer may vary. This is the first of a number of difficult questions based on specialist knowledge. Although texts exist, it is easier to ask someone.
11. 73036	zip code book telephone book	We'll need it again.
12. House of Lancaster, House of York	encyclopedia history buff history text	
13. Site of many fossils.	Encyclopedia Britannica	
14. Elizabeth Taylor	parents specialist text video shop	Again, people are the best source. They may not be reliable though.
15. 2,500 km	atlas	scaling needed very approximately
16. Gabrone	atlas year book geographic text	

17. A test of basic physical status of a new born baby performed at the birth.	mothers nurse	An extremely difficult question. Almost impossible to find in a text. Many cannot find it—but many mothers would know the answer if asked. Apgar suggests something "medical."
18. gymnastics	sports teacher dictionary	
19. Speed Rating	car dealer tire dealer mechanic	Many may guess Steel Radial. This is one of a number of questions which are best answered by phoning someone. I have always found people happy to answer such questions if asked politely.
20. milk, flour, and butter	mother or father anyone who can cook	People are the quickest source for this one.
21. oboe	musical reference musician, especially one who plays in the wind section of an orchestra	
22. light emitting diode	electrical reference electronics buff	
23. psi	back of dictionary encyclopedia specialist text buff	
24. 57,750 sq km	encyclopedia geography text	
25. Jean Henry Dunant, 1901, Switzerland	encyclopedia specialist text	
26. Aplastic pernicious anemia due to the radiation to which she was exposed	encyclopedia specialist text	
27. J.R.R. Tolkein	library catalogue keen reader	
28. Franklin D. Roosevelt	encyclopedia specialist text	
29. Burkina Faso	Britannica Year Book old and new atlas	This is an interesting one. The best method is probably using an old atlas and a new one and finding the same physical location.
30. Let the buyer beware	legal dictionary commerce teacher	
31. 1912	encyclopedia book on disasters	

32. April 19, 1995	encylcopedia yearbook newspapers	
33. varies	watch it	
34. Peter R. Kann	masthead	Note: question is "publishes."
35. -213.15° C	science teacher physics reference chemistry reference	People are easier to ask because a reference book will be hard to use unless the term "absolute zero" is known.
36. Venus	astronomy text knowledgeable buff	
37. 70 calories	calories counter	290 kJ for metric scales
38. 220.5203	library catalogue	
39. limited liability partnership	lawyer legal reference	
40. Society of Jesus, so he is a Jesuit	Catholic priest	Hard to get from a non-person reference.
41. varies	phone and ask government directory	Gives some insight using directories for government departments.
42. on the bridge (playing stringed instrument)	musician musical dictionary	Every pursuit has its own jargon.
43. varies	telephone book	government section
44. Fyodor Dostoevsky	library catalogue reader	
45. Clarke Gable	parents movie buff specialist text	
46. 99 percent	Britannica Year Book some atlases computer database	
47. Jane Austen	library catalogue reader	
48. child psychology	Who Did What? type books teacher	
49. 5362.8 people per square kilometer	Britannica Year Book (1990 year book)	worth conceptualizing
50. Jane Bennet	a guide to the book	People often guess Elizabeth.
51. 19.64 m (1991)	Guinness Book of Records – a favorite book!	

52. 75401 or 75402	zip code book telephone book	
53. someone who tried to make gold from base metals	dictionary	
54. John Ronal Reuel Tolkein	front of one of his books (inside cover usually)	
55. horse riding, shooting, fencing running, swimming	sporting reference knowledgeable person	Check that it is the *Modern* pentathlon.
56. toy dog (spaniel)	encyclopedia knowledgeable person	
57. varies	telephone book	Some prior knowledge needed.
58. varies, calculate from date of birth	recent newspaper article	
59. House of Lancaster	history book	
60. prescription drugs	pharmacist	The numbers give hazard rating.
61. 20	specialist text e.g. disasters	This proved to be very difficult. The life boats varied in size, and some were inflatable, so counting from pictures won't work.
62. 169	Chronicle of the 20th Century newspapers encylcopedia yearbook	
63. 25.3 cm	specialist text	
64. hexagonal key	most men	Appears to be a sexist question!
65. varies	telephone book	
66. lambda	back of Oxford dictionary specialist text	
67. Washington Island	atlas	
68. Pan	look at the book	Then read it!
69. double reed	musician—wind	
70. Times Mirror	small print masthead	
71. *Poor Folk*	specialist text encyclopedia	
72. bridge	card player	
73. 425	comparison of a number from several books	The rest of the number refers to the actual book code

74. 1.772 grams	conversion tables	
75. common wombat	specialist text	Not just 'wombat'—it is the common one.
76. Federal district	legal text	
77. males 35.6% females 0.5% (1987 figures)	Britannica Year Book	Interesting to compare with other countries and in terms of sexes.
78. gefallen	German/English dictionary	
79. ubiquitous—being everywhere at the same time	dictionary	
80. archaeological discoveries	Who Did What? type books	Louis, Mary, Richard are the most likely in references.
81. alto clef	musician	
82. Hera	specialist text	
83. yes, it is very tasty and non-toxic	specialist text	
84. Robert Wadlow 272 cm, 8' 11"	Guinness Book of Records	
85. National Institute on Drug Abuse	person needed	
86. James VI of Scotland who was James I of England	encyclopedia	
87. das brot	German/English dictionary	
88. It is a mangrove and needs a tidal salt water site— rare in a backyard	specialist text	
89. 55.11m (1991)	Guinness Book of Records	
90. 7920	conversion tables plus calculator	
91. a) type of French bagpipe b) air in 2/4, 3/4 or 6/8 time	musical dictionary	
92. Pierre Curie	encyclopedia	
93. Photoelectric effect	encyclopedia specialist text	

94. 7.0	Britannica Year Book	
95. 330 m/s at 0°C	specialist text	higher in higher temperatures
96. *The Gambler*	encyclopedia specialist text	
97. Io	specialist text	
98. Lasiorhinus latifrons	specialist text	
99. Henrietta Maria of France	encyclopedia	
100. 1,209,600	calculator	

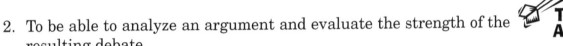

Challenge 2
Debates, Arguments,
and All-out Brawls

Let's face it—there's not much more fun to be had than participating in a good argument.

I disagree! First—what do you mean by a "good" argument? Anyway, I totally disagree with that proposition. You can't define arguing as a form of fun.

1. To develop the skills to be able to construct an argument and be conscious of both sides.

The Aim

2. To be able to analyze an argument and evaluate the strength of the resulting debate.

3. To monitor thinking in various stages associated with an argument. To monitor thinking in the various emotional states associated with different stages and different topics. To draw some conclusions on thinking in such situations.

Look through the questions in the "Thinking about Thinking Report" (question 8) so you are aware of them while completing the assignment.

Method

1. Choose a topic. You may use the list in this challenge or make up one of your own, but make sure that it is a point of view which can have two sides. For example: "Murder should be illegal" is not suitable.

2. Define the topic and write down the *exact* wording of the issue.

3. Construct arguments for *both* sides on two separate lists. Feel free to add notes on how you might counter that argument. You must look at both sides of the issue. Your resources go beyond your own knowledge and references. Other people can provide ideas as well as knowledge.

As you do this, make notes about how well you're thinking, where ideas come from, when you come up with good ideas, and how your emotional state affects your performance.

4. Prepare a strong introduction of 1 to 2 minutes for one side. Prepare to argue the topic.

5. Have the argument. Feel free to change sides and argue against your original stand if you have a good idea for the other side. Do not feel limited to only argue what you actually believe. It is the beauty of a logical argument which is worth searching for.

6. Participate in a number of other debates of the same format. A range of topics is necessary. In all cases record information for your "Thinking about Thinking Report" as you proceed with each debate. This may drive you mad, but the conclusions should be worth it. Also note your feelings about the topic. Were you passionate about one side? Did you argue just for the fun of discussion? Were you disinterested? Did this initial reaction affect the quality of your arguments?

7. Produce a report which consists of the following:
   a. The original two sides of your argument.
   b. Your opening address.
   c. A description of the argument which followed.
   d. A list of tactics for arguing well. Include examples from your argument and other arguments in which you participated, or for which you were present or have observed in the media or elsewhere.
   e. Those wonderful arguments which you thought of later (under the shower?) and could kick yourself for not thinking of at the time.

8. **Thinking about Thinking Report**
   Consider the following questions and, in responding to them, try to draw some conclusions about what affects your ability to think logically. Quote examples from the arguments to justify your responses.

   a. When did you get your best ideas?

   b. How did your thinking ability vary with each situation? For example, did you think better in the heat of the argument or in the quiet of preparation? Did this depend on the topic?

   c. How did your thinking ability vary with your emotional state? Did you argue better for the topics which you felt strongly about, or those for which you were less emotionally involved?

d. Were there any topics for which you felt incapable of arguing for both sides? Did firm views make it impossible for you to see the other side? Were there situations in which you felt others were incapable of seeing two sides? How did this affect their argument?

e. Were there any times you wished you hadn't said what you had? Did this occur in an emotional argument or in one you had little feeling for? How did the topic or your emotional state affect your performance?

f. Did the time you had to think about the argument make any difference to your ability to argue? Did this allow great ideas to form? Did it mean you became tied to one point of view? Did you enjoy the arguments more when they were impromptu or planned?

g. Did you enjoy some arguments more than others? Why? Was it the topic, the level of debate, or some other factor? Did you perform better in those arguments which you enjoyed? Does this reflect your ability to perform in subjects at school?

h. Were there students who argued particularly well? What did you like about their arguments? Were they the loudest? Did they dominate or just come out with calm, logical statements? Did they blind you with incredible knowledge? Was it something else?

i. In hearing others argue, either within your personal group or in the public arena, can you see the effects of situation, time for preparation, enjoyment, emotional state, and so on? Quote some examples.

j. How could your observations of your own thinking in these situations be applied to other aspects of your schoolwork or life?

The arguments should be conducted under conditions in which the participating group is in one of four positions physically in the room.

Methodology

These are: *for, against, neutral* (who may not participate in any way without moving to the appropriate side of the room), and the *moderator* who may not express an opinion. The neutral students are those who have yet to choose a side. The moderator is to control the whole process. All participants except the moderator are free to move to any part of the room at any time.

Every few minutes, and at the end of the argument, pause to make notes about good strong comments, why these were good, how you're thinking, your emotional state at the time, and any other notes for your "Thinking about Thinking Report."

In preparing a list of techniques for successfully arguing a point of view, consider more than just knowledge of the supporting facts. Also consider being able to conceive of the opposing view, body language, mode of speech, and tactics. Consider the following cynical approach as a starting point:

Techniques

1. Try changing the definition to suit yourself.

2. Quote "facts," e.g. 57 percent of all aardvarks over the age of 56.9 years were known to die in the 57th year. Facts work even better if they're true.

3. Insist on back-up evidence if your opposition tries the same trick on you.

4. If there is an argument you cannot argue against, get rid of it in advance using the word "naive," e.g. "It would be naive of the opposition to argue that all children are scared of the dark." It is hard for them to then make that assumption.

(Which do *not* represent the views of the author.)

Suggested Topics

1. If it tastes nice it must be bad for you.
2. Duck hunting should be banned.
3. People who are admired in society are usually those who have gained recognition due to following selfish goals.
4. It should be compulsory for every man, woman, and child over the age of 14 (junior permit age) to shoot one wild animal per week to help animal overpopulation.
5. There should be compulsory military training for all people between the ages of 18 and 26 for 1 year full-time or 3 years part-time.

6. People shouldn't eat meat.
7. "Coke is it." (Or whatever slogans are popular!)
8. You have a "good time, great taste at McDonalds."
9. Garbage collectors should put the lids back on the bins.
10. Exams should be illegal.
11. Driver's education should not be used. Drivers should go to a full license.
12. City drivers are worse than country drivers.
13. Country drivers should be permitted to drive at a younger age because they are needed to do so and gain experience around the farm.
14. Equatorial Guinea should be the political capital of the world.
15. There should be stricter measures to ensure that drugs are not taken by athletes.
16. Physical Education should be optional at school.
17. Loggers should have the right to shoot enviromental protestors on site (not sight).
18. There should be more violence allowed in PG-rated movies.
19. The legal age for the purchase of alcohol should be lowered to 18.
20. Marijuana should be legalized and should be available for purchase in the same manner as cigarettes.
21. Capital punishment should be abolished as an option for punishment for convicted murderers.
22. Corporal punishment should be permitted in schools.
23. Castration should be a sentence available for convicted rapists.
24. Einstein should not be admired as much as he is because he based all of his ideas on the work already done by Newton.
25. America should not involve itself in the problems of any country other than its own.
26. Advertisements should not be permitted on TV during movies.
27. Foxes should have a bounty put on them so hunters are encouraged to shoot them to reduce their numbers.
28. It is ridiculous for suicide to be illegal.
29. Assisting a terminally-ill person to commit suicide should be a profession carried out by specially trained and qualified people.
30. Euthanasia should be legalized.
31. High-powered guns and military equipment should be banned from private use.
32. Instead of farmers or anyone else having guns, hunting should be done by registered hunters as a full-time, paid profession.
33. Prostitution should be legal.
34. People of any religious faith have no right to approach anyone of any other belief system with the intention of converting them.

35. Exams should not be given to students below ninth grade at school.
36. Fishing is not a sport.
37. We need a world body which has the power to tell all countries what they can do in areas relating to the environment such as whaling and drift-net fishing.
38. There should be a government body which requires all scientific experiments to be approved by it so that scientists cannot follow areas of research in which the uses of their findings may not be for the good of all people.
39. Watching televised sporting events negatively affects children's attitudes towards sport.
40. Forcing students to study the classics such as Shakespeare is the only way they will learn to appreciate good literature.
41. Great spirits have always encountered violent opposition from mediocre minds. (Albert Einstein contributed this topic.)
42. Too much government money is spent on undeserving groups.
43. Social norms, such as men wearing ties and women wearing bras, are an infringement of individual rights.
44. All interviews for jobs should be done from behind a screen so the potential employer cannot make decisions based on superficial first impressions.
45. Student heroes, chosen from among their peers, are too often based on sporting prowess.
46. Politicians have a poor image which is not really justified.
47. The increase in violence on television and on videos must be related to the increase in violent crimes in society.
48. Too much emphasis is put on the need to have a college degree when it is not really necessary for many jobs available in the community.
49. People do not have the right to wear T-shirts which carry slogans that are offensive to people in the street.
50. There should be no compulsory subjects at school.
51. Grand Prix racing is a criminal waste of resources.
52. Boxing is a vulgar conflict organized by greedy people exploiting the intellectually weak.
53. Without sport our lives would be very much the poorer.
54. Sport is the natural outlet of our competitive spirits.
55. If the rules of football were tightened up enough to make the sport completely safe, it would be an absolute bore.
56. We should respect garbage collectors as much as we do doctors—both are essential to maintaining our standard of living.
57. Music is the universal language of all people.
    (Henry Wadsworth Longfellow added this to the list.)

58. Many religious leaders are out of touch with reality and, therefore, should not be viewed as having any authority from God.

59. It is necessary for a religious leader to maintain a distance from his or her flock in order to view life with clarity.

60. It is impossible for a judge or jury to decide a case without influence from their personal situations and, therefore, all legal judgments are invalid.

61. It is possible to call anything "art" these days—this degrades true art.

62. Art survives centuries while policies may last only weeks. We should pay our artists more than our politicians.

63. Too many politicians are driven by ideologies rather than facts.

64. Trying to get girls to choose mathematics and science to the same extent as boys overlooks one basic fact—most girls aren't interested in these subjects.

65. Feminists have done more harm than good for the cause of equal opportunities.

66. Without extremists, such as feminists and environmentalists, there would be no change in the opinions of people on the street.

67. In many so-called conservation protests, the participants are confusing conservation with preservation.

68. If swear words were accepted as part of the language there would be no problem with swearing.

69. The first-kiss-next-scene-in-bed images on TV and in movies undermine the choice of those people who don't wish to participate in superficial sexual encounters.

70. News and current affairs shows should be banned from interviewing anyone within 24 hours of a personal tragedy.

71. Too many journalists invade personal privacy using the excuse of "the right of the public to know."

72. The only protection we have against blatant exploitation is the threat of exposure by the media.

73. The reporting of one's crimes in the media is often punishment enough.

74. The legal system has evolved into a system which protects the wealthy from the masses.

75. People will only use public transportation to its full value when it is made safer.

76. Unions have outlived their usefulness.

77. Without unions, a minority of wealthy people will be able to rule the country.

78. Unions are a force of conservatism in the community.

79. The only people who oppose the union movement are those who are wealthy enough to not need it.

80. Unions have the right to bring down a company which it feels does not treat its employees properly.

81. Scientists are too aloof—they must be made to communicate fully with the general public.

82. Scientists have a moral obligation to follow areas of research which are deemed of value to the society which supports them.

83. We should not send aid in the form of food to third world countries—the money would be better spent on education and technology.

84. It is easy for people to talk of long-term goals and self help when looking at pictures of starving third world children—they ignore the needs of the children here in America.

85. We have no right to a second family car when two thirds of the world's population haven't yet got their first.

86. We all need a fantasy world.

87. To be or not to be—that is the question. (Shakespeare made up this topic.)

88. Sport is a health hazard.

89. The luxury of being able to oppose nuclear power is only available to wealthy countries with alternative power sources.

90. Treason laws should be abolished as they are a suppression of freedom of speech.

91. We have too many artists and writers and not enough police officers.

92. Equal opportunity is a farce—some jobs don't suit women as other jobs just don't suit men.

93. Without nationalities and religion there would be no wars; therefore, our goal should be to abolish both.

94. Smokers are being unfairly treated. A high-fat diet is known to be just as damaging to health but no one talks of banning hamburgers and french fries.

95. Keeping severely deformed babies alive is more cruel than killing them.

96. Everyone has the right to his or her own opinion, but they have no right to force their opinion on anyone else.

97. The pen is mightier than the sword.

98. Publishers should not be allowed to publish something which cannot be proven, such as fad diets and horoscopes—except as fiction.

99. Famous people gained their fame by being in the right place at the right time.

100. Breakfast is the most important meal of the day.

Teacher's Notes

Bloom's Taxonomy

This challenge concentrates on the analysis of arguments and the synthesis of cases. Analyzing both sides of an argument is often difficult, especially if the student has strong feelings about the issue; however, it is a valuable skill.

Cognitive Level

Synthesizing a logical argument for two opposing sides is a challenge worth pursuing. The actual argument is not only fun, but provides the case studies necessary for constructing the tactics and techniques section of the report. This could be seen as operating at the synthesis and evaluation levels.

The "Thinking about Thinking" aspect, or metacognosis, allows for evaluation and analysis of individual thought processes with the aim of optimizing them.

Gifted students almost invariably enjoy arguing. They like the challenge of being required to think quickly and logically. They get excited by new ideas. This situation is designed to allow them to try out new ideas, then change sides and explore the opposite point of view. Hopefully the situation will be safe enough for them to feel free to do so.

Personal Characteristics

As the topic is taken to further depths, students are able to use the talent they often possess for twisting themes and viewing them from many positions. The traits of initiative, inquisitiveness, versatility, and originality are all drawn on as the quality of debate improves. The abstract topics often appeal to highly gifted students who are able to work at a level of abstraction which is not usually presented to their age group.

Gifted students are capable of metacognitive analysis. They also seem to delight in such an analysis.

This challenge requires a group of at least six students. Some must be willing to take on the challenge of arguing for something with which they don't agree. Make it clear that there must be no quoting of opinions resulting from this situation—as no opinions expressed can be assured to be those of the speaker. This assurance makes students more

General Notes

likely to try an argument out for the fun of seeing how others react to it.

All students should be aware, in advance, of some of the other topics to be argued so that they can prepare for these debates.

"But class, you don't know what the topic is yet."

I have used a control mechanism based on something midway between formal debating and total chaos.

I let a student moderator monitor the discussion, and I change the moderator with every change in topic. I let the moderator set the restrictions (such as time limits on speakers) and choose the next speaker.

I ask the new moderator to clarify the rules when he or she takes over. I support any new rules that are put in place.

Often the moderator chooses to ban a student from the debate, especially if that student does not give the other speakers "a fair go."

I give control to any student who has been banned to let him or her see the situation from the other side. I have found that after a few such debates the moderators end up using a set of rules which is a consensus of earlier rules. They tend to adopt the same rules and students are rarely banned after awhile. I then sit back and enjoy the arguments, if I can maintain my silence. I have only been banned twice—both times quite legitimately. (But he was wrong in what he said about duck shooting!)

In situations where one student or a small group has been inspired by a topic, I have then organized larger discussions and invited an audience to participate. This has been very successful.

The metacognitive analysis has led to many great debates in itself. This challenge leads to some of the most valuable personal analysis of this type, and it is well worth spending the time to develop these ideas fully. I have often had this challenge spread over four or five weeks. Following the analysis, it is valuable to have a few more arguments and analyze these in the light of what has been learned.

The first question I often get asked with a new group is, "When do we start arguing?" It is generally the most popular assignment. This is a challenge which can be repeated often.

The topics vary from those which are quite straightforward to those which require much more imagination, such as "Coke is it." The latter often provides a greater challenge. Some topics appear to be straightforward, such as "Everyone has the right to his or her own opinion, but has no right to force that opinion on anyone else," but are in fact quite difficult.

In many cases, the argument will twist all over until firm definitions are established. Students will learn how to twist definitions to suit their own arguments. Is this a moral skill to be teaching? This would be a good topic to argue. You see, there is very little which is as much fun as a good argument.

Criteria

To what level did the student:

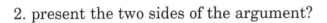

Assessment

1. define a topic clearly, including a definition of any terms within the topic which required clarification?

2. present the two sides of the argument?

3. present the opening address strongly, clearly, and with logical support for the stand taken?

4. participate in the argument, logically arguing for the opposite side to the original stand on at least one occasion?

5. describe the argument without bias in the report?

6. list tactics for competent, maybe scintillating arguing?

7. include examples drawing on the observation of, or participation in, a range of arguments?

8. present ideas for arguments which occurred after the completion of the arguments?

Thinking about Thinking Report

In the report, to what level is the student able to analyze and evaluate:

9. the effect of personal location, the time, or the source on the quality of ideas?

10. the effect of emotional state on thinking ability?

11. the effect of strong personal bias on arguing two sides of a topic?

12. the effect of the situation and emotional state on making mistakes; e.g. statements made in the heat of the moment which were later regretted?

13. the effect of allowing ample time for preparation on the quality of the argument?

14. the effect of enjoyment of an argument on performance?

15. the performance of others?

16. the application of these observations to other aspects of schoolwork or life?

Challenge 3
Show Me You
(and the universe and an atom)

You are between one meter and two meters tall.

If I drove at 100 kilometers per hour for an hour, I would travel 100 kilometers.

If I drove at 100 kilometers an hour for 16.7 days, I would travel around the world. (Note, I have an amazing car which can travel through any medium and on any surface.)

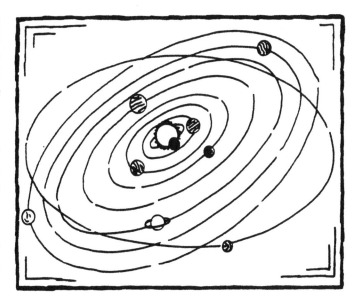

If I drove at 100 kilometers per hour for 160 days, I would reach the moon, which is about 384,400 kilometers away.

If I drove at 100 kilometers per hour for 63,400 days, I would reach the sun (our nearest star).

Our solar system is 11,000,000,000 kilometers across.

If I drove at 100 kilometers per hour for 14 million years, I would reach the next nearest star. That star is about 4 light years away. (A light year is the distance light travels in 1 year at 300,000,000 meters per second. So a light year is about 9,000,000,000,000 kilometers.)

The super nova which we all got so excited about (well, some of us did) in 1987 is 170,000 light years away. So the star, now named 1987A, exploded 170,000 years ago, but the light from the explosion only arrived in 1987 so we knew nothing about it until then.

The furthest galaxy which we can see with the naked eye is about 2.2 million light years away—the Andromeda galaxy.

There are more figures in the getting-bigger scale.

You are between one meter and two meters tall.

You are made up of cells which range in size between 5 and 40 micrometers. A micrometer is .000001 meters. That's the size you started at.

Cells are made up of atoms which are about .0000000001 meter across. That's not very big. How many atoms, approximately, would you have in you?

Atoms are nearly all empty space. The nucleus, the middle bit, is only 1/100 000th of the size of an atom although it is almost all the mass.

Elementary particles are smaller—they make up the nucleus.

But you are between one and two meters tall.

All I want is for you to represent these concepts in a visual form. Maybe a poster. Maybe successive pages. Maybe some other way which you see as being appropriate.

The center point, the focus, the base—is **you**.

The aim is to present yourself relative to an atom and to the universe. And while you're doing it, keep some notes on how you're thinking, when and where you got your great ideas, and so on.

You will need to find out facts and figures which I haven't given. You might like to include the population of your city, then country, then the world. You may like to go in numbers of cities, countries, planets, stars, and so on. Any logical progression is relevant.

You might like to include a theory on the likelihood of life on other planets given the number of stars in the universe. You may wish to present your results philosophically, e.g. "Am I insignificant in the light of the nature of the universe and atoms?"

Or then again, are you an incredibly unbelievable

being made up of so many billions of atoms connected in such an extra-ordinary way?

This concept may send you into an image completely different from any of these: you are different from all the other 5,500,000,000 or so people in the world. Aren't you?

The ability to present your response to such information and to communicate it to others is the basis of your assessment in completing this challenge.

Who or what are you relative to life, the universe, and everything—even an atom?

Make sure you include both ends of the scale!

"Self Portrait"

Teacher's Notes

Bloom's Taxonomy

This challenge emphasizes the synthesis level of the taxonomy. There is some analysis required within the interpretation of data, but the importance of this challenge is to ask students to form a link in the scale, be it philosophical or physical, and create a way of putting their ideas together to communicate their concept of themselves in this context.

**Personal
Characteristics**

Gifted children are often noted for their ability to conceptualize. They like to create their own theories and explore reality. Creativity is also, at times, quoted within the definition of giftedness. It may be that the situation for children to demonstrate their creativity may not have arisen. An ability to do "art" well is far from a full definition of creativity.

Being able to present such concepts in a visual form means the student must fully understand what he or she is trying to convey. Some time spent in preliminary activities is valuable. Playing with the numbers as a group or discussing ways of approaching the task is useful. I have suggested to students that they try to avoid forming an idea for their approach until they have spent some time browsing through books—on astronomy, atomic structure, atlases, or encyclopedias. In doing this, most students found that the way they wished to proceed became obvious.

Monitoring this browsing process in terms of creativity is fascinating. The two have often been linked by "great achievers."

Gifted children are often characterized by an ability to see relationships more clearly and earlier than their peers. They often possess an unusual imagination or ability to approach a problem in an individual way. High levels of moral, emotional, and philosophical development are often noted.

It is these characteristics which are being addressed by this challenge.

Thinking about Thinking

This challenge is asking for a creative approach to the representation of the self. In contrast to the logical approach being taken in challenge 2—Debates, Arguments, and All-out Brawls—this challenge is asking for a gentle, individual response.

Again the monitoring of the thought processes involved will lead to valuable discussion and note-taking. The notes will be useful for the comparisons which can be made between the observations of metacognosis from the contrasting assignments.

The response may be quite emotional yet a different type of emotion to that aroused in some of the debates. A class discussion of the outcome of the monitoring leads to some fascinating observations.

Gifted children vary greatly in the talents which they display. They may not have developed a talent for which they have potential. This challenge is designed to allow a range of talents to be displayed. It is possible to complete the task in a number of ways depending on the individual tackling the assignment.

**General
Notes**

Teenagers are beginning to go beyond a purely physical and present self-concept. This area is more pronounced in very bright children. Even less mature children may enter this cognitive phase early when they are of high intellectual ability. Although this challenge can be tackled from a purely mathematical approach, it can also be extended into the area of self-concept and personal relevance. Introducing population figures or other statistical data could be valuable. I have noticed the fascination gifted students have with statistics.

There are two excellent resources for this challenge. The first is *Asimov's New Guide to Science,* by Isaac Asimov. I have the 1987 edition, but it is continually revised. The second is the *Encyclopedia Britannica Year Book* which is a gold mine, especially the back section which contains an incredible array of statistics about every country.

Higher-level thinking skills are differentiated from simple memory tasks by the need to make connections and see relationships. This is an ability which can often be neglected in a classroom where most students are required to complete the set tasks. This challenge relies on a significant ability in making such connections.

The presentation of this assignment is an area of importance and I would suggest allowing some time to mull over the concept before starting on the final product. If possible, a trip to an observatory would be invaluable. I have been amazed at the effect that seeing Saturn in all its three-dimensional glory can have on a student. Similarly, being let loose with a powerful microscope would act as a valuable stimulus. A combination of both, within hours of each other, could have a profound effect.

A philosophical discussion on the relevance of an individual is also valid in the initial stages. I discourage students from finalizing their approach to the presentation until these avenues have been explored a little.

Bias the discussion if necessary. I do not want any child to come to the conclusion that he or she is irrelevant!

Assessment

Criteria
To what level did the student:
1. present the ideas and information clearly?

2. use the visual form effectively?

3. focus on the personal individual?

4. synthesize a role relative to a larger scale, such as the universe?

5. synthesize a role relative to a smaller scale, such as an atom?

6. integrate information from other sources, such as references?

7. display originality and creativity in the synthesis of these ideas and the information?

Thinking about Thinking Report or Discussion
To what level is the student able to analyze and evaluate:
8. his or her emotional response to solving the problem?

9. his or her intellectual response to the problem?

10. the process and the way in which the resulting visual form developed?

11. the difference in personal thinking in the long-term individual project when compared to the argumentative situation (if completed following "Challenge 2—Debates, Arguments, and All-out Brawls")?

• •

Challenge 4
Blinding Blurb

1. To learn to judge whether jargon is unintelligible because of your own lack of familiarity with the product range or whether it is deliberately blinding.

The Aim

2. To gain the confidence to admit when you don't understand particular information and ask for clarification.

A friend came to me with an advertisement. She claimed it was totally unreadable:

Challenge Blurb

> "Computer. PC compatible, 386/40, Super VGA, color, DOS 5.0, 80 Mb HD, 101 keypad, 4 Meg RAM, 387 Co-pro, 3.5 in floppy, s/w included. $1,700"

> "Sounds good to me," I said.

She showed me another advertisement which she was more interested in, being in the process of house hunting:

> "Old World charm:
> Superbly loc DF timber home, spac lng, main bdrm BIR's OFP, modern bthrm, 2nd bdrm OFP, large sittingrm OFP, tiled kit with WO, HP, rangehood and dbl SSS. WWC. 2 bedrooms (ES to main). Ample BICs. Will be a beautiful home with some TLC."

"Great," I said, "the only bits I don't understand are those which follow 'superbly'. Is WWC something to do with toilets?" She wasn't impressed, being completely familiar with the jargon herself.

So I spent the morning searching papers, magazines and the back of packets and bottles. Here's a sample of what I found, with the product names omitted to protect the guilty:

• •

A perfume ad: a "chemise of fragrances, provides a liaison between skin and clothes. Becomes a woman's lifelong way of scenting—resplendent, clinging, never turning against her."

A company which "brings you" Something, "a beautiful jewel for lovely lashes. A beauty treatment for tired eyelashes that contains lipo-vitamins to condition and lengthen every lash."

Tired eyelashes? Hmmm ... My dictionary had a lot of lipo-things but none of them were lipo-vitamins. 'Lipo-' is a chemical prefix meaning 'fat'. Does that help you?

A Bio-energenic, Anti-fatigue Absolu is explained: "The Energesium microcapsules release their energy-releasing forces, diffusing them deep within the epidermis. The result: the skin is recharged with essential energy; the complexion is renewed with infinite radiance. Don't try to live without it."

Absolu?—I really must get a new dictionary. I couldn't find Energesium in any chemistry books, but a physicist was very keen on the idea of infinite radiance. This product apparently leaves the sun for dead as a producer of light! As for energy releasing forces—what are they? "Energy forces" are favorites with ad-pseudoscientists. I just don't know what they are.

"Hydrolyzed Human Hair Keratin Protein to seal and strengthen, Aloe Vera to replenish moisture, Allantoin for healthy scalp and a synergistic blend of natural oils in a substantive cationic base."

My dictionary has "synergistic"! Try reading some of the research on Aloe Vera if you want a story of a marketing miracle with no scientific backing.

Car ads are always informative:

"All new MH Triton V6 4 X 4 standard cab chassis. 3 lt V6, 5 speed manual, ECI injection, power steering."

It just didn't say what it was exactly—a spaceship, maybe?

"Falcon. XF 86 S-pack 4.1 EFI auto 4-whl dsks, A-C, P-S, centr lock, c-control, white, 10 mths reg, RWC."

I know what "white" is.

Then I got to the Public and Legal Notices, some of them saying I could object in writing to the subject of the notice within 14 days. It would take me that long to translate the ad. Then the legal ones. (I'd love to go to a party of the first part, but I never get invited to this type.) Some of the personal ads for new "friends" were very vague. I decided that maybe I preferred them this way!

The job ads were interesting. A recession brings out the shonky dealers. Or is he a serious, bone fide business?

"SIMON SAYS
Simon says are you motivated?
Simon says can you demonstrate?
Simon says we will train you.
Simon says earn what you want.
Simon says do not delay ...
Simon says ring if you dare.

Phone Simon on *** ****"

Am I supposed to demonstrate 3-in-one vegetable splicers or demonstrate against war? Earn what I want—really? Millionairedom here I come!

Then there was the ad for a workshop—advertised mid-November, which stated:

"It's time to 'heal your life'; to let go of the struggle and pain; to gain a new lease of love and power; overcome personal and career setbacks; to create the happiness and success you deserve;
AND DO IT ALL BEFORE CHRISTMAS. Phone *** ****
to be part of this life enriching process."

All these ads are genuine. But are they all legal?

Challenging Minds

Method

1. Try to translate my little collection. Find someone who knows the jargon, and see how much they can help.

   You may prefer to construct your own translation first before investigating the genuine meaning. I dare say your version will be far more imaginative.

2. Collect a minimum of 10 ads in which the text is not immediately comprehensible. Translate these to the best of your ability, using whatever experts you can recruit.

3. Choose an approach to take this further:
   a. Present a broad view of the use of jargon in advertising, distinguishing between ads which use jargon to convey technical information to those who use it to blind the reader. Analyze the technique and its application to the advertising industry.
   or
   b. Specialize in learning to translate a particular type of ad, such as cars or computers or real estate. Analyze the technique and construct a dictionary for those who wish to read these ads. Include euphemisms, e.g. "a tradesman's dream" may be translated as "a total dump."
   or
   c. Go beyond the advertising world to other areas which use the same technique: health cures, wine writers, art reviewers or any other realm in which the writers use their own jargon to blind— whether deliberately or not. Create a dictionary for those wishing to interpret articles written in this particular genre.

4. Include in your report a sample of such ads or articles, large enough to illustrate the points you have made in your report. Include references in an appendix. Make sure your references include people, their authority, and *exactly* what they said in transcript.

5. **Thinking about Thinking**
   How did your thinking affect your ability to complete this task? In particular:
   a. Did you find a problem approaching companies to explain their jargon? Can such discomfort impede your progress on such a task?
   b. Did your previous knowledge have an impact on your ability to interpret the advertisement?

c. Did your familiarity with the jargon affect your degree of suspicion? Were you more skeptical about ads with which you were less familiar?

d. How could these reactions influence your thinking in other aspects of your life? For example, do you distrust people who are using jargon you don't understand?

e. Do you see evidence of this in others? Do scientists distrust artists while artists distrust scientists due to a language problem? Justify your response to this and add other relevant examples.

Teacher's Notes

Cognitive Level

Bloom's Taxonomy

There is obviously a degree of knowledge and comprehension in this challenge. There is a great deal of work at the analysis level and at the evaluation level. It is for the students to judge whether the use of jargon is necessary to provide the required information or is there to confuse.

Students who produce a dictionary or guide to the translation of the jargon are working at the synthesis level.

Personal Characteristics

Again, this challenge involves a degree of humor. A student with a particularly creative sense of humor could do very well creating a translation which will amuse you. Hence the addition of the second part of method point 1.

Gifted students often enjoy obscure facts, display curiosity and inquisitiveness, and may be very interested in the nature of language. Through this challenge they could develop an interest in the abuse of language!

General Notes

References to the use and abuse of jargon are becoming more common in the press. Some books are also being published on the area. An example is *Skin Secrets* by Dr. Peter Berger (Allen & Unwin), published late 1991. This serves to start the attack on advertisers and pseudoscientists using jargon or fads to sell products.

Similarly, some students may wish to pursue this investigation through the legal avenue. *The Law Handbook* will give students the relevant law (which is not impossible to interpret). However, it does appear impossible to apply. I have discussed this aspect with a number of lawyers and members of the police force who all state it is a very difficult area of the law to enforce.

You will find the jargon-packed beauty product ads in expensive magazines which seem to consist more of ads than anything else. Sleazy ads are more common in the mass market press, while the oddities are usually found in magazines. "Legalese" is found in abundance in any of the

Public Notice and Legal Notice sections of the newspapers. The For Sale section, especially of smaller local papers, can be very interesting to read.

Wine reviews are common and easy to find, but the best jargon is in the more up-scale publications. Psychologically-based ads ("Subliminal methods to improve your psychomotor level of consciousness"—again a direct quote) are common in magazines aimed at the "alternative" section of the population or the Arts section of newspapers.

Art reviews are found in many more up-scale journals and are often the brunt of jokes, as are the film critiques. It would be a worthwhile exercise to have an interested student write to the reviewer, or an expert in the field, to question the actual meaning of the article. It may well be that the student will discover a real meaning to the review and a deeper understanding of the art work or film.

The same approach could be applied to any of the advertising agencies or product manufacturers. The back of shampoo bottles, make-up products, and health food can all be useful. Cleaning products, electrical goods, and pseudo-religious objects are also invaluable. Then of course, there are the football reports! All of these writers of jargon could be asked to simplify their text for a polite student.

I have found cosmetic companies, in particular, to be most responsive to students. My students have been surprised to find that many examples of ads which they were suspicious about were, in fact, bona fide, and they gained the confidence to ask for clarification when people responded positively to their polite inquiries.

For reasons of good manners in writing to such people, the assumption of all students should be that the jargon is accurate and legitimate unless there is good reason to judge otherwise.

Challenging Minds

Assessment

Criteria

To what level did the student:

1. present and translate a sample of the genre?

2. select a logical approach to the challenge and proceed accordingly?

3. use resources fully to maximize understanding of the genre?

4. present a report which clearly explained the use of jargon in the genre of choice?

5. reference the sources of information?

Thinking about Thinking Report

In the report, to what level is the student able to analyze and evaluate:

6. the effect of discomfort (or lack of it) when approaching people or companies for information?

7. the impact of previous knowledge on interpretation of advertisements?

8. the effect of familiarity with the jargon on the level of suspicion of the honesty of the advertisement?

9. these effects in other aspects of their lives?

10. the effect of language differences in how much people distrust others in society?

Challenge 5
Nourish and Flourish

You are going to open a restaurant in a standard sized shop in your town or suburb.

You need to fully plan the venture. The task is based on your ability to identify the type of information you will need and find a way of getting it.

It is all just a matter of priorities! What is more important? Money, time, space, quality, wide range, innovation, decor, staff, facilities, or position?

You need to plan on making a profit!

Part A: Analyze the Competition
Based on past experience or present research (go and eat!) compile a list of the aspects involved in running a restaurant. Exactly what needs to be considered in setting up such a venture?

Try to separate each of the areas (menu, site, staff, money, etc.) and detail the aspects that need to be considered in each. Try to note the links between the individual aspects that create the entity, i.e. the restaurant business.

Prepare such a list with examples drawn from at least one restaurant.

Then, think about your own venture. As you do so, try to identify your priorities and how you came to such a decision. Was it based on logic, experience, someone's opinion, or some other value?

So:
   Is it to be haute cuisine which costs a fortune for a minute but fashionable dish?
   Is it to be massive servings of greasy french fries and tough steak at low prices for the thronging masses?
   Is it to be cups of tea in china cups with dainty iced cakes in a quiet atmosphere?

Is it to be Coke and hamburgers in an environment with blaring heavy metal music for the in-crowd?

And:
Is there to be a board on the wall?
Is there a handwritten menu re-done daily depending on seasonal foods?
Is the menu to be printed with straightforward dishes, e.g. hamburger with the lot?
Is the menu to be artistically designed with names that require an explanation in small print below to save the server explaining the entire selection?

Will you:
Provide toilets?
Have plenty of waitresses and waiters?
Serve alcohol?
Have someone wash the dishes?
Be open on Sundays?
Allow live bands to gain exposure?
Pay large amounts of money for well-known entertainers?

Will it have:
Pink curtains?
Mirrors to make it look bigger?
A menu in the window?

"The service isn't bad, but I particularly like what they've done with the decor."

Carpet?
Dead flies?
Customers?

Will it be called:
Bill's Burgers?
Sheridan's?
101 High St. (Behind the grocery store)?

Will you:
Have 200 T-bone steaks in stock, in case everyone wants them, and throw out 198 at the end of the week?
Use frozen stock?

Will it ...

Part B: Prepare a Report

Your report should include at least:

1. A floor plan.
2. A menu.
3. An approximate budget.
4. An idea of how you will decide on and manage stock.
5. Proposed staffing.
6. Justification for your decisions on *each* of the above.
7. Possible problems.
8. Decisions which will have to be reviewed after some experience in the restaurant business.
9. Problems that you had in preparing such a plan.
10. Any regulatory bodies and legislation of which you need to be aware.
11. Sources of information.
12. Whatever else is needed for a complete report.

You are going into business for yourself. You can do anything you like, as long as you aim for a profit. Have all the current food presenters missed out on some great idea? Have you always said, "Why don't they ...?" This is your chance!

Part C: Trial Run

Test drive your model. Run through, in writing, what you would imagine to be a typical week for your restaurant. In doing so, keep track of your staffing, customers, orders, stock, costs, and time commitments. How does it look?

As a result of having seen what the others have produced in attempting this challenge, write a constructive criticism of your own presentation.

Thinking about Thinking

How do we decide on priorities? Why does everyone come to a different final design? Try to analyze how you came to your priorities and compare this with others.

Teacher's Notes

Cognitive Level

Bloom's Taxonomy
Students are expected to analyze the various aspects which make up a restaurant. They should be able to see the various interlinking facets of such a business. They should also analyze the limitations the need for the business to be profitable places on the service which can be offered.

The synthesis aspect involves the design of a restaurant based on the guidelines having been formed from the analysis stage. The degree of complexity will depend on the ability of the student and the time available.

Evaluation can be done by test running, in theory, their own model. This type of method is often referred to as "desk checking" a plan. If the assignment is being done in a group, comparisons (of a constructive criticism type) with the plans of other students is a valuable exercise.

Personal Characteristics

This assignment is based on developing ideas from common experiences. Very few students haven't eaten in restaurants. Very few haven't used or been associated with some small business venture. The natural curiosity of gifted students and the tendency to analyze daily experiences is addressed.

Gifted students see relationships between variables more easily. A restaurant is more than just food. It is a complex relationship between the purchase, preparation, serving, and budgeting around the common factor of food. It involves advertising, rates, situation, decor, and so on. Seeing these relationships and working with them is the basis of this task.

Students of high potential also often possess fertile imaginations. Some may like to take this assignment out of reality. Some may like to use their imaginations to develop a feasible and original concept. As a group, they should be able to see the value of combining individual talents.

General Notes

A great excursion idea: as a group, go to a restaurant, or send droves of students to a range of restaurants! Or enhance family relationships by requesting parents to take them to a restaurant.

The emphasis within the report will depend on the talents of the students. Some will prefer to concentrate on the more aesthetic concerns while some will get involved in the budgeting. They should use their particular talents while being encouraged to consider the other aspects as well.

I have run this exercise in the form of designing a school, a restaurant, and a hospital. The degree of difficulty increases in that order.

The school designs tended to reflect the present school, but are easier due to the experience the students have. The budget was one of the few difficulties, but as most people employed in schools are on fixed wages, this proved reasonable. The students were shocked at how much it costs to run a school. They also all wanted to add horse-riding as an extracurricular sport.

The restaurant proved a little more difficult, but was much easier for those who had a contact, or made one, with someone in the industry. A guest speaker could provide this link. (If promised a group booking, the enthusiasm of the speaker could be enhanced!) Priorities vary. One student allowed 10 toilets for a restaurant seating 30 customers. He hates waiting in line for a toilet.

The hospital design is very complex; the first step involves organizing wards and nurses. Then the reality of cleaners and catering and counseling and maintenance and TV repairs and pharmacy and ... sets in. This is a major task for a group of highly motivated students living near a compliant hospital. We were supplied with the complete budget for an enormous local teaching institution which fazed most of the class. There were a few, however, who were fascinated by the statistics and complexity of the institution. The analysis stage is probably more relevant than synthesis, in this case.

It is valid to get involved in regulations, politics, unionism, and many other aspects of such a venture. Advertising is worth considering, as are environmental aspects. Students can follow many aspects beyond the immediate assignment.

If this project is being done by a group, it is useful to consider whether various members of the group could work together on the report by choosing aspects of the restaurant and becoming specialists. In this way you can have students using their own talents to enhance the project. A clear understanding of specific responsibilities is essential. If not, there will be plenty of material for later evaluation!

Challenging Minds

Again, encourage students to use as wide a variety of resources as possible—especially people.

Assessment

Criteria

To what level did the student:

1. create a useful and comprehensive list of considerations from observation of existing restaurants?

2. identify the desired business and priorities within it?

3. analyze reasons for the choice made?

4. prepare a clear design?

5. prepare a comprehensive design?

6. justify decisions made?

7. consider both the financial and aesthetic aspects of the design?

8. analyze decisions which will need to be reviewed after the restaurant has opened?

9. analyze problems encountered in designing the restaurant?

10. include details such as government regulations, legislation, council by-laws, and so on?

11. cite sources of information?

12. document a theoretical trial run?

13. constructively criticize the design?

Thinking about Thinking Report

In the report, to what level is the student able to analyze and evaluate:

14. the thought processes involved in the completion of this task?

15. the priorities established?

16. the effect of these priorities on the final design?

17. the way in which the priorities became established?

18. the way in which others established priorities and the effect on their designs?

Challenge 6
Hero Worship
(or: Elvis Presley is better than Albert Einstein)

All right, so you admire Albert Einstein more than anyone else in the history of the universe. All this theoretical physics stuff is all very well, but, frankly, who cares?

Now, Elvis Presley—he's a different story altogether. He gave enormous amounts of pleasure to millions of people. Thousands of us got fit jumping about to his music. He provided pictures with which to adorn many

a teenager's wall and even old people (some over 30!) thought he was great. The money didn't matter to him. He did it all for his fans. Anyway, only a few ever read anything of Einstein's. I think Elvis is far more worthy of my admiration than Albert.

Then there's Mother Theresa. It's easier to do good when you've got thousands of poor people hanging around than it is to make it into the pop music industry and stay at the top for years. She only did it so she could go to heaven. That's selfish. Elvis did it all for us—his fans! Elvis is the King!

—L. Visfan

This admiration caper is rather interesting. Why do some people gain the respect, admiration, adoration, praise, devotion, esteem, acclaim, homage, allegiance, and worship of others? And are these all the same anyway (despite what the thesaurus says)?

It's time to have a look at this hero business and find someone who is worthy to be your hero.

1. Whom do people admire and why?

    A good starting point would be to find out who makes it into the admiration stakes. Come up with a list of at least 20 names from a simple survey and give reasons why people admire the people that they do. Categorize the "heroes" and write a general analysis of what you've discovered.

2. Whom do you admire and why?

Now, the time has come to see if there is someone whom you could really admire and who stands up to some testing. Choose someone— or a few people. Research their achievements, personal backgrounds, and, if possible, their motives for following the course they chose. In your report, provide the background information, assuming the reader knows nothing of this person. Then justify your choice of hero.

If you are part of a class, try to justify your hero to the group. Question their justification and accept questioning of yours. Avoid the knock-the-tall-poppies syndrome, but expect a thorough justification of any choice.

3. While you're in those biographies, try to find out a bit about your hero at your age.

Was she or he popular at school? From a young age, did he or she show signs of the qualities which you admire? What was this person like?

4. Do people need heroes?

Do we have a need to have people to admire? Why do people adore certain film stars or become fanatical about religious or political leaders? Are there many "little" people more deserving of our admiration?

Look at people's behavior in this respect and write a response to the question from your personal perspective. As this is a personal view, as long as your justification is reasonable, it is (by definition) correct. However, discussing your view with others will be worthwhile—but think about it yourself first.

Support your opinions with anecdotal evidence.

Some interesting case studies to consider are:

Jim Jones—who led his followers to commit mass suicide in Guyana in 1978. Nine hundred thirteen people died, including 276 children.

Adolph Hitler—and his ability to inspire his followers to commit such horrendous crimes.

The story of Rasputin and the Russian royal family.

The status of Albert Einstein—who is so often seen on posters and so often quoted.

The status of Mother Theresa and her ability to inspire hope.

The fanaticism of political followers during an election. (If you can arrange to have a major election occur, it would be most useful!)

The adoration of whatever athlete happens to be a "sports star" at the time of the project.

Do people need someone to admire for some reason?

Thinking about Thinking

How did you search for a hero? Did you mentally sift through a data-base? Did you use references, hints, or clues from others?

In justifying your hero, did you react emotionally to the arguments? Is it important to you to have such an idol? Many people report great dis-appointment if someone they have greatly admired is shown to be less than worthy of admiration. Could you feel this way about your hero?

Others report disappointment if they cannot find someone to admire. Are role models the same as heroes, and do we need them in some way?

Did others defend a hero in a way which you felt was beyond logical acceptance? Do people believe what they want to believe about their idols? Can this cloud judgment in some way?

For example, political leaders sometimes have followers who accept every word they say even if they contradict a previous statement. Is hero status a license to use undue influence? Are there examples of fanatical adherence to the words of a hero in current news items?

Teacher's Notes

Bloom's Taxonomy

This is a much shorter assignment—which I have found necessary as a break from the very long ones—which works at the evaluation level. It requires students to make judgments about the motives and achievements of others. They are working at the synthesis level when creating the support for their choice of hero.

Cognitive Level

The last section is to introduce students to abstract philosophical thought and to the value of their own observations of, and opinions on, human behavior.

Gifted children are often great observers. They note human behavior and the incongruity in it. They often show interest in the feelings and emotions of others. They are also known to have very high expectations of themselves and others. Hopefully this assignment may assist with being realistic about such aims. Gifted children are reported to have a keen interest in the motivations of others and a highly developed sense of moral and social responsibility. This assignment allows them to investigate such interests.

Personal Characteristics

I have usually asked students to jot down 10 names of people they admire or would consider "heroes" before I hand out the assignment. I usually get a collection of sporting and theatrical stars. I collect these lists for later distribution. Their final lists, as requested at the end of the assignment, are usually quite different. They have a clearer definition of "admire" and of "hero." I give back the original lists.

General Notes

Classroom discussions have often taken the form of debates as to the worthiness of the hero. I had one student choose a tennis star, and I immediately attacked her choice on the grounds of the player's blatant self-interest. Her entire argument was based on his sportsman-like behavior on court, in comparison to his peers, and the example he set for younger players. She won!

The response to thinking about the way we think about heroes has led to many observations of groups which appear to behave illogically or fanatically in the following of a hero. Interesting debates on the thinking of mass followers, of which there are usually some examples in the news, have resulted. It can be a sobering way to look at human intellect.

I have some idealized idea that asking students to consider what behavior is worthy of admiration is a way to help them analyze their own goals in this light. Hopefully, this may form a part of their decision making for the rest of their lives. Well, I said it was idealized!

The research part of this project is difficult. There is usually no lack of information on people's achievements, but their motivation is also relevant here. This is where the difficulty arises. Some students have chosen people they know well, which has proven easier in the motivation area but harder in terms of achievement. Assignments based on the students' own parents have often been extremely rewarding for all involved.

This form of research, e.g. the reading of letters and biographies, is valuable and goes beyond the standard gathering of facts.

As to the philosophical third part, I have often wondered about this point, having become depressed myself when someone I admire greatly is found wanting. I have also often been amazed at the willingness of people to admire someone proven less worthy. Many past crimes are ignored.

It is important to avoid anecdotal material from films and novels. These characters are fictitious—yet students often quote them as examples. They can be used well as scenarios but not as supporting evidence.

Some of the best assignments have been based on people who are not famous but are related to the students or are personally known to them. This is a pleasing result!

Criteria
To what level did the student:
1. design and run the survey of people's heroes?

Assessment
2. analyze who people admire, and why, within the limitations of the survey?

3. prepare a biographical report on a chosen hero or heroes in terms of admirable qualities?

4. justify the personal choice of hero?

5. (if in a class) justify the chosen hero to others and respond to questioning?

6. report on the chosen hero as a child and teenager?

7. present a hypothesis on the reason people need heroes?

8. evaluate human behavior in terms of the choice of heroes?

9. support and justify the hypothesis and opinions presented?

Thinking about Thinking Report

In the report, to what level is the student able to analyze and evaluate:
10. the way in which the hero was chosen?

11. the effect of emotional response to the hero on evaluating worth of admiration?

12. personal need for, and response to, a hero?

13. (if in class) the choice and justification by others of their hero?

14. the role and influence in society when considering this emotional effect on the way people think?

Challenge 7
Laughable Logic

Good English has went.

MyagorophobiaissostrongthatIhavetoavoidallspaces.

If at first you don't succeed—so much for skydiving.

Those of you who think you know everything really annoy those of us who do.

He who laughs last probably didn't get the joke.

What's wrong with political jokes? They get elected.

Brain: the apparatus with which we think we think.

Spelling a word the same way all the time is a sign of a pathetic lack of imagination.

Isn't it strange—the same people who laugh at gypsy fortune tellers take economists seriously?

Logic: going wrong with confidence.

A wet pelican walks with a stilted gait but a dry fish swims alone.

• • • • • • • • • • • • • • • • •

Deep, very deep, but funny? In fact were any of these funny? If so, why?

It is easy to laugh, but not so easy to know why we are laughing. It is even harder to actually express in words what it is that makes something funny.

In order to control knowledge, and locate it again, it is necessary to classify. Librarians classify their books while zoologists perform a similar process on animals. We're going to classify humor.

This challenge is to try to define and classify humor.

Method

Step 1. Examine classification systems. The most familiar would be those mentioned—animals and books. Bar coding systems for products in supermarkets are a form of classification. It is necessary to classify a charge or crime before it can be decided which law applies and which court is to try the charge.

Using a number of classification models, assess what basic steps are needed to set up a key allowing an item to be classified. A key is a document which lets the user take the item to be classified and, usually through identifying continually more detailed characteristics, end up with a full classification. This is to the "species," not to the individual.

The question: How do I set up the classification so that someone else can use it to classify an item in their hand when that item is funny?

For example, I have the video of the greatest piece of humor ever produced: *The Hitchhiker's Guide to the Galaxy*. I need a classification system which allows this to be labeled appropriately. Is the starting point my (indisputable) opinion of the quality of the humor, or the fact that it is in video form, or that it was originally a book written by Douglas Adams, or that I first saw it on November 9, 1987, at 7:45 p.m. in my mother's den?

I can see problems with all of these starting points. Is there a starting point which doesn't cause some problem, or do we choose the best, not the perfect, one?

Step 2. Look at as many examples of humor as possible. In doing so, draw up a list of groups of examples.

Watch, read, listen to, and look at as great a range as time permits.

Thinking about Thinking
In doing so, spend some time monitoring your thinking. How easily are you distracted by enjoying the actual item, and, there-

fore, distracted from your task? Can you optimize your ability to concentrate on the task at hand?

The more examples you have considered before you design your system, the more likely your design will fit the range.

There must be a time limit. This step could take the rest of your life!

Step 3. The range—that's a problem. Was that last political broadcast technically "humor" or not? Personally I found it hysterically funny, but I doubt it was intended as such. Then again, I saw a comedy sketch last week which I found offensive and refused to watch. The next sketch was boring, but the guy next to me was in hysterics. Therefore, what is included?

You will need to define "humor" in order to clarify the bounds of your classification system.

Consider:
Is wit different from humor?
Are spoken comments humor?
Does it matter if it is on some recorded medium?
How vulgar are we going to allow humor to be before it becomes smut? Or is smut legitimate humor? What about pornography?
Do we include irony or sarcasm?

It may be interesting to conduct a survey to collect showing what things amuse different people. Try to analyze your results according to age, gender, occupation, education level, and any other factors that you would consider relevant. Do you need to allow for this variation in designing your system—especially if there is one person doing the design of the classification key? Could personal bias enter into the classification? It should be eliminated in a well-designed system—even though this isn't easy to do!

Out of interest, compare Dewey's numbering for geography. Note the range of numbers given to areas and cities in the U.S.A. compared to the rest of the world. Compare the numbering for the Christian religion compared to all other belief systems. Dewey was classifying from within a Christian American viewpoint. Is it desirable or even possible to classify from a totally objective viewpoint?

Step4. Design a classification system for humor. It must be in a format which can be used by someone other than yourself. Construct a usable key for applying your classification system.

It must aim to be unbiased. (Except, it should clearly show *The Hitchhiker's Guide to the Galaxy* as vastly superior to all other humor, unless you can justify any other inferior view.)

Thinking about Thinking

Try to keep track of your thought processes as you design the system. How does your mind decide what is a useful approach? How does it refine the design? Or do you prefer to adjust your interpretation of the humorous item to fit into the classification? How flexible are you?

Step5. Test your system. Ask some unsuspecting person to choose any five pieces of humor. You should do this without him or her having any knowledge of your classification. Ask him or her to classify the items he or she chose according to your system.

Thinking about Thinking

How do you react to problems with the design? Why do you react as you do? Does this reaction affect your ability to optimize the design? Are some people better at accepting constructive criticism than others? Does the style of the speaker affect the way in which you react to criticism?

You may find that you are satisfied with the system; if so, justify your satisfaction with further trials and documentary support.

If you find the trial indicates areas for improvement, continue to optimize your system until you are satisfied or time runs out.

Step 6. With your report containing your classification and supporting evidence, include an evaluation of your approach and system. Is it based on a sound definition? Is such a thing possible? What problems were encountered? Could you have approached the task in a better way? And so on.

And, by the way, the answer to the Great Question of Life, the Universe and Everything is 42. (*H.H.G.T.T.G.*)

Step 7. This humor stuff looks pretty simple. Now try writing some!

Sorry—my bias: Now try writing/drawing/telling/filming/sculpting/recording/singing/performing some!

Step 8. Look back at your ideas on the three "Thinking about Thinking" sections, and see what conclusions you can draw about your own reaction to distractions, flexibility and response to criticism. In discussing these concepts, look at how they apply to other aspects of your life. Also consider the influence of these factors on others—especially those in the public arena.

Teacher's Notes

Bloom's Taxonomy

Classification is one of the major areas of the analysis level of the taxonomy. Classifying humor is extremely difficult. It is also fun. Creating the classification key and the required definitions falls into the synthesis level. The classification is then applied to samples of humor.

Cognitive Level

You may not be surprised when I mention the trait of gifted students to exhibit a developed and often warped sense of humor. This, however, will need to be viewed in such a light when developing a key to be used by all people. This challenge also appeals to the natural tendency to organize information and the ability to handle higher levels of abstractions than other students.

Personal Characteristics

No, I don't understand about wet pelicans and dry fish either, but it sounds good.

I have found the easiest definition to use is one based on the intention of the item. If it was intended to be funny or was seen as such when presented (for example, a film of someone tripping over accidentally), then I have included it. There is scope for much more inventive definitions.

General Notes

This challenge is best done individually. It is valuable, and fun, to view the items as a group. This also allows for the collection of a far wider sample for analysis. The discussion of the items, in terms of classification, is also valuable, initially, in a group situation. However, synthesizing a key in a group, even a very small one, seems to be far less efficient than an individual effort due to the complexity of the task. The person designing the system needs to have the overview in mind. Students seem to work with a logic that they are often not able, at least initially, to put into words. For this reason, individual work has proven to be more successful; however, try both methods so that students can discover the alternative route.

The presentation of such a key is also individual. Classifications vary from purely textual approaches to highly graphic layouts.

Looking at existing systems initially is invaluable. The two mentioned are the most readily available. The key for the Dewey library classification system is published as "The Dewey Decimal Classification System" and comes in three expensive volumes. These can be found in the library but are almost certainly not for loan.

Animal and plant classifications are readily available. Biology teachers are sure to have various examples. The entire animal kingdom is a massive classification. The animal section by itself is enormous. A subset, such as birds, mammals or reptiles, is easier to handle. Similarly with plants, a single class of plants is easier.

The classification levels used for living things: kingdom, phylum, class, order, family, genus, and species is an excellent example.

The main difficulty with this assignment is getting past the stage of telling jokes, watching videos, and exchanging cartoons. I have found it best to do some of this and promise more after we start the classification analysis. Then a second viewing allows students' ideas to be further developed. Again stopping, with the promise of more, to begin the design of the key, enables the assignment to progress. A third break and viewing, with the keys in hand, is valuable. The assignment then progresses through both aspects.

In "Thinking about Thinking," one crucial observation is that of how to maintain concentration on a given purpose in the presence of a Great Distracter—such as an uproariously funny video. The role of distraction in achieving a goal should be discussed. This can vary from the favorite—blaring radios while studying—to unavoidable aches, noises or little brothers.

The second issue is the actual mental mechanism of humor. Why do we laugh? Can you monitor your mind while it is assessing some input to decide if it is funny or not? I have found the humor is often lost if you try.

Third, how did students come up with their classification system? What mental tracks did they follow? Were some more successful than others? This is a case where students have reported a try-it-and-see mechanism, continually refining their classification system or throwing it away and starting again.

The major complaint about this assignment is when I interrupt a humorous interlude with, "Now stop for a moment; why did you all laugh at that? Why was it funny? How would you classify it?"

The last stage of producing humor will need to be developed depending very much on the individuals in the group. There are cases where parallel approaches of classification and creation would be valid. That will depend on your classroom management and assessment of the personal talents and interests of the students in the course.

It is essential that anything produced be treated with constructive criticism. Good humor is close to impossible to create. Humor which everyone finds funny is impossible. There are even people who find *The Hitchhiker's Guide to the Galaxy* dreadfully boring. Oh, well.

Criteria

To what level did the student:

1. clearly define humor?

2. define the bounds of the classification key presented?

3. synthesize a classification for humor?

4. explain the classification and how to use it?

5. use objective classification terms so that the user does not make judgments about the "funniness" of the humor?

6. test the classification key and report on the results of the testing?

7. evaluate their own classification key when completed?

8. use supporting evidence to show the adequacy of the classification for a range of items?

9. produce a sample of humor?

Assessment

Thinking about Thinking Report

In the report, to what level is the student able to analyze and evaluate:

10. his or her ability to deal with distraction?

11. the way in which the design of the classification was developed?

12. his or her flexibility in adjusting the design once established?

13. his or her reaction to the testing stages of the design and any criticism which may have arisen at that stage?

14. the effect of the above factors on other aspects of his or her life?

15. the effect of the above factors on other people in the way they behave?

Challenge 8
A. A. Milne—Poet or Psychic?

I have always known that A. A. Milne's book of children's poetry *When We Were Very Young* was of special import, and now I can reveal why. It is really a subtly disguised set of psychic predictions.

Naturally, I have not yet managed to interpret all of his quatrains, septrains, octrains, and fifteentrains, but I have deciphered a sufficient number to give proof of my claims. Move over, Nostradamus.

First, A. A. Milne not only predicted the computer age long before its advent, but even exhibited the computerologists' trait to blind bias to a particular brand:

> John had a
> Great Big
> Waterproof
> Mackintosh-
> And that
> (said John)
> Is
> That.
>   *—Happiness*

His future preference for the Apple Mac is clear and unbending.

He even details the peripherals we attach to the computer:

> What shall I call
> My dear little dormouse?
> His eyes are small
> But his tail is e-nor-mouse.

Note his reference to the lack of eyes on the mechanical mouse, but the long tail—the lead connected to the machine.

As an Englishman, it is no surprise that most of his political references were to his own country. In this same poem, he goes on to tell us about Britain's Prime Minister, John Major:

I sometimes call him Terrible John
'Cos his tail goes on–
And on–
And on.

Well, he is a politician, after all. Note the very clever play on the word tail/tale.

And I sometimes call him Terrible Jack
'Cos his tail goes on to the end of his back.

Is this predicting that his speeches will one day be used to knife him in the back? Watch—I guarantee this will come to pass.

And I sometimes call him Terrible James
'Cos he says he likes me calling him names ...
—The Christening

Here we have clear reference to the slightly masochistic nature of anyone who would choose to be a political leader with the behavior of parliament and the British journalists being what they are.

Milne makes many clear political comments on recent events in the international arena, of which he could have had no knowledge. I will include but a few.

Take the following reference to events which have occurred in the former Communist block (behind the Iron Curtain). The "Red" reference is obviously the Communist link. He refers to the attempts of a reformist, obviously Gorbachev, who wasn't quite Red, nearer Brown; his meetings with Margaret Thatcher, referred to as Nanny; then his sudden departure.

Note the implications upon the skill required to negotiate with him. As you read, take time to enjoy the references to the previously aloof nature of the Russian State, and its recent allowance of Western visitors. I did enjoy his dig at what happens to Reds who get "browned off" and their subsequent rapid and often violent departure from the scene.

In the corner of the bedroom is a great big curtain,
Someone lives behind it, but I don't know who;
I think it is a Brownie, but I'm not quite certain.
(Nanny isn't certain, too.)

I looked behind the curtain, but he went so quickly –
Brownies never wait to say, "How do you do?"
They wriggly off at once because they're all so tickly
(Nanny says they're tickly, too.)

"Nursery Chairs" uses the imagery in a particularly clever way to predict the Falkland's battle between Argentina, here referred to by the continental reference of "South America," and Britain, represented, as always, by the lion. Note the inference of restraint on Britain in terms of the full flight nuclear attack of which it is capable. The naval nature of the battle is beautifully contrasted to the position of the rest of us in the "Me" reference.

One of the chairs is South America
One of the chairs is a ship at sea
One is a cage for a great big lion
And one is a chair for Me.

He so clearly predicted the Falkland's Battle, and then went on to describe the Gulf war:

I'd sail my ship
Through Eastern seas
Down to the beach where slow waves thunder–
The green curls over and the white falls under–
Boom! Boom! Boom!
On the sun-bright sand.
                    —*The Island*

The predicted victory of the green garb of the Western armies over the white of the Iraqis should have been reassuring to the Allied forces.

A.A. Milne was clearly aware of political events and wars to happen long after his death. He was obviously predicting events of the time in which we now dwell. Were these references just proof of his abilities to force me to listen to his warnings?

I am now in a state of pure panic! A.A.M. has sent a crucial message. He has been forced, by the severity and sensitivity of the mission, to resort to code. He has been too cryptic for me! James James Morrison Morrison Weatherby George Dupree is so obviously an alias; it is too ridiculous a name to be otherwise. A clue. The crucial verse is even headed with a note of the form:

(Now, then, very softly)

What else could this imply but the need for secrecy. It goes on:

> J.J.
> M.M.
> W.G. DuP.
> Took great
> C/o his M*****
> Though he was only 3.
> J. J. said to his M*****
> "M***** " he said, said he:
> "You-must-never-go-down-to-the-end-of-the-town-if-you-
> don't-go-down-with-ME."

How much clearer can he make his warning of the dire consequences which will obviously befall M***** if I don't stop him or her going down there alone? I must find out who J.J., M.M., and W.G. DuP. are.

Marcia, Manuel, Marina, Marcus, or Matthew—I'm coming!

Challenge: Psychic Milne

The Aim

1. To develop critical skills when arguments are based on quotations taken out of context.

2. To develop the skills to become suspicious, check the original, and evaluate the conclusions drawn on the full text.

3. To become aware that too much suspicion destroys a learning opportunity.

Steps

1. Read the above document and absorb its implications. Go back to the original and see if the author has been in any way selective in the quotes chosen. Explain your conclusions.

2. If you have access to the claims of Nostradamus, investigate them and see if you can draw any conclusions as to whether they are more realistic than those interpreted by the author for A. A. Milne. Try to

· ·

find a copy with the original French quatrains and see if that makes any difference to the interpretation.

3. Find a poet, any will do, and from within his or her poetry find quotes which can be used to prove that the poet had prophetic powers. Produce a document, at least as convincing as that on A.A. Milne, to back your claim.

4. Take today's newspaper. Find at least *three* examples of arguments which have been put forward based on comments taken out of context. See if you can check the way in which they were selected. Can you see a problem with performing such a check? If so, is this in some way able to be exploited by the press? If not, how often do people perform such checks?

5. Can you create a plausible original conversation from which the quotes could have been taken? In this original, make the intention of the speaker quite different to that which was implied by the writer of the article.

   Write out the conversation between the interviewer and the interviewee as it could have happened, giving the quotes used in the article. Make the comments actually mean something quite different.

6. Could this method of deliberate misinterpretation also be used by other members of the community? Give examples of how and why this could be done.

7. Could we become overly suspicious and therefore reject valuable information? Give at least three realistic, hypothetical examples to support your contention.

8. What conclusions can you draw from this exercise? Do you have any suggestions to assist those listening to or reading the media?

Thinking about Thinking

Consider the following questions for discussion:

1. This assignment encourages you to be silly, to have fun, and to play with ideas. How does this mood affect your thinking?

2. Do you need to concentrate as hard in completing such tasks as you do in activities such as solving a complicated math problem or puzzle?

3. Did the theme ever enter into other activities? For example, did you ever twist the meaning of an activity to create something different? Did you question quotes taken out of context when not specifically working on the assignment?

4. Do you feel your responses to this activity were more creative than they would be to a task which did not involve your sense of humor (or is it more a sense of the ridiculous)?

5. In accepting or rejecting information, how much of your behavior is a response to logical evaluation and how much is due to you believing what you want to believe? Are some people easier to deceive than others? How does your mind work when given new information? Does your level of suspicion depend on whether you want to accept or reject the information?

How does this influence our lives? Is it more relevant to belief systems than science? Is there an opposite effect, i.e. people believing anything if it's in a book or on a computer?

How does your initial opinion of information affect your thinking?

Teacher's Notes

Bloom's Taxonomy
This assignment is designed to extend skills in the areas of analysis and synthesis. Evaluation of the claims of Nostradamus and sources of quotes is also involved.

**Cognitive
Level**

The assignment is designed to allow students to use the humor so often associated with gifted people. These traits include the tendency for an unusual sense of humor as well as a developed sense of the ridiculous. They are often quoted as having a curiosity about the more unusual aspects of our society.

**Personal
Characteristics**

I have found that gifted students have an acute interest in controversial claims such as those related to psychics. They are rarely given time or a methodology to evaluate these for themselves. It is important that the teacher does not take a strong personal stand on the validity of Nostradamus. It is the methodology for evaluation which is being developed in this exercise. Then again, the teacher may choose to take such a stand, on either side, to argue with students, encouraging them to make a rigorous response.

**General
Notes**

If the assignment is being used in a group situation, a classroom debate would be of value.

Some students have not yet discovered the delights of Milne. These poor, deprived souls are in a situation which must be remedied immediately.

Question 7 must be given full due. We accept most information without question. This is one of the faults of most education systems—we train students to do just that. But, it is also a danger to train them to demand so much confirmation that valuable time is wasted. Discussion of this theme is worthwhile and links with the discussion of the "Thinking about Thinking" ideas.

Challenging Minds

Assessment

Criteria
To what level did the student:
1. explain the author's selective use of the poems?
2. produce a logical claim to the psychic abilities of the chosen poet?

3. select quotes from a newspaper or magazine which may have been taken out of context?

4. evaluate the probability of being able to check the validity of the quotes?

5. create a plausible original conversation which contains the quotes?

6. use the quotes in a way that gives an impression quite different from the original presentation in the newspaper?

7. evaluate the possible use of deliberate misinterpretation by members of the community?

8. evaluate the possibility of becoming overly suspicious?

9. draw conclusions from the exercise?

Thinking about Thinking Report
In the report, to what level is the student able to analyze and evaluate:
10. the effect of playfulness and light heartedness on his or her thinking?

11. the need for concentration?

12. the relevance to other aspects of his or her life?

13. the link his or her own creativity has with tasks involving humor?

14. his or her own ability to evaluate information depending on the desire to believe?

15. other people's ability to evaluate information depending on the desire to believe?

Challenge 9
Photocopying Mirrors

Once upon a time, I was teaching a perfectly good lesson on nuclear decay. The students were writing notes and peace reigned. I was praising myself on my class control.

"I think I'll do my project on how photocopiers work," said Aaron. "Great idea!"

I was encouraging, as all good teachers are, "and the alpha decay occurs when ..."

"I could get a picture of the insides of the photocopier by photocopying a plane mirror, couldn't I?" Aaron again. "It would be like a photograph of all the works and then ..."

I gave him one of those withering teacher looks guaranteed to silence any student. He mouthed, "Sorry."

I returned to the lesson confident of the complete attention of my class: "Alpha decay is the result of ..."

"It wouldn't work! The light would be reflected back and it'd just be white like a sheet of paper." Cameron was as taken with my lesson as Aaron.

"No," called Brian, "it'd work a bit, but with ..."

"Let's try it!" Aaron enthused as he and Cameron headed for the back cupboard and left my room with a large mirror. Half the class left with them. Class control has never been my forte, but it's usually better than this.

I was attempting to enthuse the remaining students with a topic which I find rather fascinating—alpha decay—when the phone rang. It was the librarian:

"Your students are in the library trying to photocopy a mirror. Are you aware of this? And to make matters worse—they don't have a permission slip."

I replied: "Yes, of course I gave them permission. I have total class control. I sent them up there to ... um ... photocopy a mirror because ... It won't happen again." (I will try to justify blatant lying some other time.)

My students returned with a set of photocopies. They showed a dark space—the size of the mirror. Thin white lines in the space were compared with the mirror and found to match the scratches and finger prints on the surface. A clean mirror photocopied totally black.

"Great," I said, "you can work out the explanation of that over lunch. Now, alpha particles ..." and I managed five minutes of absorbing lesson.

"We might have overloaded it," said Cameron. "I wonder what would happen if we used a small mirror," and my classroom emptied completely.

The librarian called: "They're back again—and they still don't have a permission slip."

Argument reigned in the corridors and on the playing field. Everywhere the words "photocopy" and "mirror" could be heard, echoing in the halls of knowledge. Well, nearly.

Two weeks later the distressed librarian called yet again.

"Did you know that your students are photocopying an old cardboard box? Inside it has writing on a bit of paper suspended at different heights." She added, "And they don't have a permission slip."

P.S. I have reviewed the way I teach alpha particles. I will do better.

Challenge

The above is a true story—even the names are correct to convict the guilty. Since that moment I have witnessed arguments between physics teachers, students, photocopy technicians, and guests at a 21st birthday party. I still do not have a conclusive answer.

Why does a mirror photocopy black? The way to get a totally black image is with the lid open, allowing all the light to escape. Place a white sheet on the copier, and you get white. The light is being reflected back. The original logic was that a mirror would reflect the light back and so the image, if not of the insides of the copier, would at least be white.

By the way, the librarian has been seen photocopying mirrors.

And while you're playing—see what fantastic artistic creations you can come up with photocopying curved mirrors, lenses and anything else which comes to mind.

Include these to make your report a truly beautiful document!

Thinking about Thinking

As in all great scientific work, many of the ideas, of what to try and how, come at specific times. Can you identify the situations which appear to be conducive to the good ideas?

Do you give up at the first hurdle or does difficulty inspire you to move on? How does this aspect of your approach reflect in other aspects of your life?

Did you try using a variety of resources: books and people? When? Was it when you were short on inspiration, or at the start, or some other time? What pushed you into broadening your perspective to include the ideas of others?

Do you have an independent streak? Was this activity a puzzle, a challenge to be solved alone? If so, why did you choose this path, and was it a good choice?

Have you any other observations to make on your methodology and thinking in completing this task? How do all these aspects relate to other tasks you undertake (or reject) and how could you optimize your ability to solve such problems?

Teacher's Notes

Cognitive Level

Bloom's Taxonomy
This one uses the lot: knowledge, comprehension, application, analysis, synthesis, and evaluation are involved to a significant degree.

Personal Characteristics

Although this seems to be a straightforward challenge with a closed response, it proves to be otherwise, as the challenge is in the experimental design. Academically strong students base their skills on a strong knowledge base. They are all familiar with photocopiers. They are all familiar with mirrors. They probably haven't put them together. The expansion of the application of familiar devices will appeal to students who enjoy knowing how things work.

Intelligent students enjoy a challenge. They are stimulated by an experience which does not match the logical prediction. This activity is also within their ability to solve.

General Notes

This is a more straightforward challenge, with a fairly linear problem-solving strategy required; therefore, any skills learned from pursuing this task will be invaluable in many aspects of education. The "Thinking about Thinking" discussion can be used to look at general problem-solving techniques.

Hopefully, students will have learned from the 100 questions task that their resource base is far wider than textbooks. The images produced from the photocopiers have also been artistically beautiful.

I also learned a lesson from this challenge: students come up with better challenges than I do!

The result of this assignment was a set of posters from Cameron and Aaron explaining their very convincing argument. Their "conclusive" evidence was found by photocopying the box ... so we thought.

They concluded that a photocopier works with a minute depth of field.

This is compared to a camera which uses a larger one that allows the background to be seen.

The image of the object is the same distance behind the mirror as the object is in front. The image of the light source, which the machine is trying to photocopy, is about 10 centimeters behind the glass. By photo-copying a note on a white piece of paper at distances retreating from the glass surface, they could show that the image soon disappeared and the white paper photocopied as black. This matches the familiar experience of losing the words to darkness when a very thick book, which will not lie flat, is photocopied.

A jubilant pair of students produced their report. A group of physics teachers lost half an hour at a meeting designed to assess the posters as they argued the truth of the students' conclusions. They failed to agree after another hour's argument over lunch!

We have since had a letter from a photocopy technician stating that the students' conclusions were correct. We have also had an equally conclusive let-ter from a different company stating they were completely off beam. (Sorry, I liked the pun.) The second technician stated the reason for the black image had to do with the position of the detector which is narrow and assumes diffuse reflection, while a mirror produces specular reflection and, therefore, the light does not reach the detector as it is reflected at an angle.

I have another physics teacher claiming that the overload theory still has merit. I am enjoying the controversy and wish it a long life!

The students sidetracked a great deal in their research, and we learned a lot about method. They tried:

1. Curved mirrors, which added to the confusion.

2. Lenses, which added more confusion, and were soon eliminated as not much help but very pretty.

3. Laser photocopiers, which were sure to produce a different result. Why, I never did quite understand, but there was no doubt in the experimenters' minds. However, they did prove that laser light behaves as light! The result was the same, but colored.

4. Big, small, overlapping, closely spaced, round, square, and broken

mirrors—all were tested. Theories about contrast became popular at one stage. A teacher at a neighboring school suggested that the machine was being overloaded. More experiments.

5. Quizzing everyone available: physics teachers, older students, parents, technicians, and letters to photocopy manufacturers.

(I had one father beg me to tell him the answer before his daughter destroyed his company photocopier. He was distressed to find I didn't know. What sort of teacher doesn't know the answers to problems posed? I tried to explain I hadn't posed it. But I would have if I'd thought of it!)

They also had a great deal of fun. An offshoot was the art student who picked up the image from one of the concave mirrors as a design basis.

And the answer? I still don't know for sure. I like the depth of field solution, but I think the position of the detector is more likely to be the final answer. In fact, I am actually nearly convinced. Oh, well.

This problem is particularly suitable for use with an individual student or a small group of students. They will rope in others, anyway.

This task involves all the cognitive levels as defined by Bloom. It is also a very good exercise to give a gifted student with a particular interest in physics. Photocopiers involve a great deal of physics and provide a readily available, but stimulating, device to explore. It is also a great way to get such a student to play with lenses and mirrors and explore the ray traces thoroughly.

The actual physics required for the solution is quite simple, just reflection in plane mirrors.

As to my not giving a conclusive answer: I intend to remain unconvinced as long as possible. Students delight in the fact that I have set an assignment to which I don't know the answer. This is not common in schools. I explain that I am capable of setting an infinite number of assignments to which I don't know the answer—far more than those to which I do. But they like this one. So do parents. I have a photocopy of crumpled up aluminum foil from a father who is also a scientist. It was very pretty, but he hasn't given me a conclusive answer yet. By the way, his son was two grades lower than those who were tackling the challenge. They were getting anxious, and he was very bright so they thought he was worth a try!

Criteria
To what level did the student:

1. design an appropriate investigation for the problem?

2. propose a realistic hypothesis?

3. support the hypothesis with evidence and logical arguments?

4. use resources, including people, to assist in the investigation of the problem?

5. display persistence—i.e. avoid either accepting the first hypothesis which occurred or simply giving up?

6. present the hypothesis and supporting evidence in a clear manner?

7. play with the problem?

Assessment

Thinking about Thinking Report
In the report, to what level is the student able to analyze and evaluate:

8. situations in daily life which appear to be conducive to producing good ideas?

9. his or her response to difficulties?

10. his or her use of resources?

11. his or her tendency to independence, or otherwise?

12. the way in which he or she could optimize his or her ability to solve such problems?

Challenge 10
Dare to be Different:
A Hypothesis

Before I propose my hypothesis, I would appreciate it if you would complete this exercise:

1. List 20 famous people alive today, as well as the talent for which they are famous.

2. List four names for each of the following domains: music composition, music performance, singing, painting, dancing, science, mathematics, writing, team sports, individual sports, leadership, drama writing, acting, directing, or porducing.. Two names should be people who are alive or who have only recently died. Two others should have accomplished their achievement before 1850.

You may ask other people for help.

The **Enduring** Achievement Hypothesis:
Great achievers, whose fame endures long after their deaths, are those who dared to be different.

Corollary: Those who are famous, or achievers in ways which do not lead to enduring fame, are those who comply with accepted norms. They may be considered different to much of society, but will conform to a group within it. Those who so conform, such as sporting heroes, pop stars and actors, are more likely to achieve fame and fortune within their lifetime than those who dare to be different. However, their fame will not last beyond a generation or two.

A Case Study: M. C. Escher

Marits Cornelis Escher produced wood- and lino-cuts which displayed exceptional originality. His work defied reality while appearing to conform to it—waterfalls which flow uphill and staircases which descend to their own starting points. He melded shapes of fish into those of birds and played with space, time, and impossibilities in ways which fascinate his legion of fans. Posters of his prints probably outsell most other artists. Born in 1898, he will, without doubt, endure and grow in fame.

This Dutch artist attended the School of Architecture and Decorative Arts, Haarlem, when he was in his early 20s. His official report said of him: "he is too tight, too literary-philosophical, a young man too lacking in feeling or caprice, too little of an artist." His set work was not highly regarded by his examiners and he was poorly rated as a student.

In his book, *The Magic Mirror of M. C. Escher,* Bruno Ernst says, "Until recently almost all Dutch print collections had omitted to build up any fair-sized section of Escher's work. He was simply not recognized as an artist. The art critics could not make head nor tail of him, so they just ignored his work. It was the mathematicians, crystallographers, and physicists who first showed great interest" (p. 15).

He goes on to say: "Now that the tide has turned and the public at large seems captivated by Escher's work, official art criticism is bringing up the rear and showing an interest. It really was quite pathetic to see how, on the occasion of the great retrospective exhibition at The Hague, held to commemorate Escher's 70th birthday, an attempt was made to establish historical parallels. It did not succeed; Escher stands apart. He cannot be slotted in, for he has totally different aims from those of his contemporaries" (p. 16).

If greatness in art involves being widely appreciated and drawing people into appreciating art who would not normally have done so, there can be no doubt as to Escher's achievements.

● ●

Not all people who will be famous for centuries are deserving of praise. For example, the Marquis de Sade is not widely admired, but he is widely known. The fame of Adolph Hitler will continue in the same way. They did, however, dare to be different.

The following is a list of famous people who may appeal for study.

Note: These are all people who have achieved *enduring* fame, or are pretty likely to do so. Hence the sample is biased in terms of evaluating the hypothesis. Or is it?

Jane Austen
Charles Babbage
Johann Sebastian
   Bach
Lord Baden-Powell
Josephine Baker
Ludwig van
   Beethoven
Sarah Bernhardt
Henry Bessemer
Otto von Bismark
Niels Bohr
Johannes Brahms
Benjamin Britten
Lewis Carroll
Paul Cezanne
Charles Chaplin
Winston S. Churchill
Christopher
   Columbus
James Cook
Marie Curie
Gottlieb Daimler
Charles de Gaulle
Rene Descartes
Charles Dickens
Fyodor Dostoevsky
Thomas Alva Edison
Albert Einstein
Dwight D.
   Eisenhower
Queen Elizabeth I
George Elliot
Ralph Waldo
   Emerson
Michael Faraday
Gustave Flaubert

Alexander Fleming
Henry Ford
Francisco Franco
Sigmund Freud
Gandhi
David Lloyd George
George Gershwin
Ernest Hemingway
Edmund Hillary
Adolph Hitler
James Joyce
Helen Keller and
   Annie Sullivan
Franz Kafka
Immanuel Kant
Johannes Kepler
John Maynard
   Keynes
Nikita Sergeyevich
   Khrushchev
Rudyard Kipling
Thomas Edward
   Lawrence (of Arabia)
Lenin
Abraham Lincoln
Charles A. Lindbergh
Joseph Lister
Ada Lovelace
Guglielmo Marconi
Karl Marx
W. Somerset
   Maugham
Golda Meir
Lise Meitner
Robert Menzies
John Stuart Mill
Louis Mountbatten

Benito Mussolini
Isaac Newton
Friedrich Nietzsche
Florence Nightingale
Alfred Nobel
Lord Nuffield
Blaise Pascal
Louis Pasteur
Pablo Ruiz Picasso
Marco Polo
Cecil Rhodes
John D. Rockefeller
Auguste Rodin
Franklin D. Roosevelt
Theodore Roosevelt
Bertrand Russell
Ernest Rutherford
Albert Schweitzer
Joseph Stalin
Margaret Thatcher
Mao Tse-tung
George Bernard
   Shaw
Leo Tolstoy
Arturo Toscanini
Mark Twain
Vincent van Gogh
Guiseppe Verdi
Queen Victoria
Richard Wagner
H.G. Wells
Oscar Wilde
Christopher Wren
Frank Lloyd Wright
Wilbur and Orville
   Wright
Sun Yat-sen

Method

1. Define the terms used in the hypothesis.

   If a class is working on the assignment, try to come to some kind of consensus within the class. Record the definitions and check them every now and then to remain conscious of them. If necessary, negotiate a refined definition; but if you do so, write down why you felt this was necessary.

2. Investigate, in detail, the achievements and personal characteristics of one famous person.

   You can use one of those on the attached list. If you wish to investigate someone else, arrange to do so—just check that they comply with the definitions decided on previously. Remember the hypothesis is dealing with *enduring* fame, not just any old flash-in-the-pan celebrity. The more people doing a different study, the more detailed data available for the discussion (debate, argument, or all-out brawl) later.

   In doing so, find out what you can about the person as a child. Was he or she happy at school? Did he or she show early signs of future eminence? Did he or she have a mentor of some kind? Was he or she popular, "well-rounded," sociable? Did he or she do well at school in terms of achievement in examinations? How did he or she achieve their success?

3. Investigate, in brief, as many others as possible within the time limit.

4. Accept, refine, or destroy the hypothesis.

   Whatever you choose to do with my precious hypothesis, please do so with logic! Avoid deciding on its validity based on whether you would like it to be true or not.

   or

   Propose your own hypothesis.

   If your research has led to other ideas, propose a new hypothesis or a corollary to this one, and support your hypothesis with facts and logic.

5. If you are working in a class, use the methods developed in "Debates, Arguments, and All-out Brawls" to gain a consensus view.

Provide a brief report of such a discussion including references to areas of agreement and areas of diverse opinion.

6. In your report, include:

   a. Your detailed biographical notes.

   b. Your brief biographical notes.

   c. Your conclusions with respect to the hypothesis, and your reasons for drawing those conclusions.

   d. Any notes on discussions, comments from other people, or ideas for future study, which are relevant.

Teacher's Notes

Bloom's Taxonomy

This assignment is mostly directed at the analysis and evaluation levels. It is to be hoped many students will take up the challenge of creating their own hypothesis and testing it, which is part of the cognitive activity of synthesis. Obviously there is a degree of knowledge, comprehension, and application involved as well.

Cognitive Level

Gifted students are known for their curiosity. Many show great interest in biographical data, and this assignment is designed to expand that existing interest or introduce students to it.

Most students also try hard to fit in with their age peers. The need to be accepted is part of human make-up. It may be helpful to those who find this difficult to read about role models who had the same problem. It may also help some gifted students realize that being different has some advantages, too, and assist them in rationalizing this aspect of their personalities.

Personal Characteristics

Thinking about Thinking

No section for monitoring thinking is included. The reason is to have students look back and see how conscious they have become of their motivation.

Ask them to look back over their thought processes in following this investigation. How much was the search for information based on a desire to prove or disprove the hypothesis? How much was this desire a response to how much the student originally wanted to accept or reject the hypothesis?

Did any students actually perform the research with an "open mind" and then evaluate the hypothesis as a result of their findings?

Students should discuss these issues and look at the effect of thinking processes on other aspects of their lives. For example, what gossip do we accept without investigation when we want it to be true? Similarly, how hard will we (or the media) hunt for "dirt" to knock down a tall poppy?

This discussion can be related to "Challenge 8: A.A. Milne—Poet or Psychic?"

General Notes

I chose the 150-year timespan because it goes beyond the memory of anyone still living and, therefore, the person will have been discussed or read about outside family recollections.

I came up with one pretty old sports hero: Archer, who won the Melbourne Cup in 1861 and 1862, but he was a horse.

I have rarely found a bright student who was not fascinated by Escher. I encourage you to encourage your students to become familiar with his work—if they have not already done so.

The range of pursuits of those listed is enormous, and students should be able to find someone on the list who worked in an area which matches their area of interest. This is appropriate for the study of one person in depth. Other people should be chosen in different fields of achievement. Of course, students can change the hypothesis and limit it to a single cognitive domain if this is more manageable for them.

The reading of biographical information is a popular pursuit with gifted children. To get enough data in a given time, it is better to use more potted forms of biographies than full texts on a single person. Those I have found particularly good include:

1. Encyclopedias, especially the *Encyclopedia Britannica*.

2. Biographical dictionaries, such as *The Biographical Dictionary of Scientists*. There are four volumes: *Astronomers, Biologists, Chemists,* and *Physicists*. Similar publications are available in other areas.

   More general biographical dictionaries, such as *Who Did What?* are a good starting place. This one has more than 5,000 entries. It also has a fascinating "time chart of human achievement" as an appendix.

3. Collections of potted biographies, such as *100 Great Modern Lives*, edited by John Canning (1972); published by Souvenir Press. There are others of this ilk. These have more detail than many encyclopedias, usually giving 4 or 5 pages per entry.

With this starting point, students may find a desire to go to greater depths and investigate more detailed biographies. Some students have wanted to find out more about the teenage years which usually requires an extensive biography. This may reflect a need to reassure themselves about their own social position.

The list of famous people I've provided can be used in a number of ways. Students can choose those which they would like to investigate further. Alternatively, the teacher could allocate a given number to each student in the class, giving a wider coverage and less bias in selection. This list is not exhaustive. Its creation naturally involved some selection. By adding to it you or the students will reduce the bias in that creation process.

As indicated in the heading to the list—these people have achieved enduring fame. In order to fully evaluate the hypothesis it is logical to say that others have to be studied to see if the reason their fame didn't endure was due to conformity. This is a harder project—but a valid, and possibly essential, one.

The hypothesis is vague, therefore, clear definitions of the terms are required. It is arguable whether someone like Madonna or Elvis Presley dared to be different or whether they differed from the mainstream but fit in with a subgroup of society. But then, that's what evaluating a hypothesis is all about.

I have been fairly well convinced by one student that the nature of media is more important. She argued that enduring fame cannot exist if the medium required to record the achievement in its original form is not available. Hence, the recording of written and artistic achievements predate the recording of sporting and musical performance.

Another student argued enduring fame results from having something named after you, or from somehow becoming a "household" name.

Maybe there's a combination of ways to achieve enduring fame.

References which may be of interest:

Ernst, Bruno. *The Magic Mirror of M. C. Escher,* Ballantine Books, New York. First published in English in 1976.
Locher, J. L. (Ed.) *The World of M. C. Escher,* Harry N. Abrams, Inc., publishers, New York. First published, 1971.

Challenging Minds

Assessment

Criteria

To what level did the student:

1. define the terms used in the hypothesis given?

2. investigate great achievers and draw out relevant features of their lives?

3. present the biographical data?

4. present an argument for the hypothesis, against the hypothesis or for an alternative hypotheses?

5. use biographical details to support the argument?

6. (if in a class) contribute to the debate on the hypothesis?

7. (if in a class) report on the discussion giving alternative views?

8. conclude the argument?

Thinking about Thinking Report

In the report, to what level is the student able to analyze and evaluate:

9. his or her own tendency to search for biographies which would support a desired stand on the hypothesis?

10. the selective reporting of information which matched a desired outcome?

11. how openly they accepted information which may have contradicted their desired hypothesis or stand on the hypothesis?

12. the implications of searching for knowledge when looking for a particular point of view?

13. the implications on what information is accepted when looking for a particular point of view?

Challenge 11
Problematic Probing

To discover a way to gain information about a sensitive issue in a way which can then be analyzed.

In particular, answer the following question:

The Aim

What do people believe about God and why?

There are some steps to use to help you prepare and successfully complete this challenge. These are suggested and may be adjusted after negotiation with your teacher.

Method

Step 1. Collect survey results from newspapers and magazines, and use these as a guide throughout the assignment. You may wish to contact a professional survey company for results. They may be willing to give you any guidelines they use in surveying sensitive issues. You may wish to include an appendix in your report of such items with your own comments on them.

Step 2. Take a safe issue to gain experience in designing, running, and analyzing a survey.

Try to find out who people follow in football and why. If interviewees don't like football, ask them why.

Use a smaller sample, say 20, just to test your techniques. Prepare a rough report, including any problems which will help you in your next survey.

Use the *considerations* given below as a guide—but only a guide.

Step 3. Try a more sensitive issue. Find out how your selected population feels about our political parties and their leaders. This time, try to ask the range of questions which you think will give interesting feedback. You may wish to increase your sample size depending on how many people you see as necessary to show the response clearly.

Step 4. Tackle the real question. As this is no longer a trial, you will need a larger sample size. You will need to design questions which lead to data that can be analyzed and allow you to draw a conclusion.

Most Importantly

You must do so while respecting people's right to privacy. Should there be an easy "out" for people who don't wish to respond? If so, how will you deal with such people in the analysis? If not, are people who do not wish to respond going to be honest?

Step 5. Having completed the final report, include a further comment on how well you feel your results can be relied upon and any other comments you wish to make about researching issues which are considered private.

Considerations

1. What should be considered in designing a survey so the results can be analyzed?

    a. You will find that vague questions lead to vague answers which defy statistical analysis.

    b. The way in which you want the question answered must be clear, e.g.:

    > List your preferences from 1 to 10.
    > Choose only one response.
    > Write anything you want.

    c. How will you decide which options to include in a multiple choice answer?

    It is a common practice to interview a small number of people in the form of an open question (e.g. "What do you like doing on weekends?") to get a list of responses. This can avoid the problem of personal bias in choosing possible responses.

d. Make it clear whether you require a name or not.

e. Ensure constant format, e.g. age: 24
24.3 (24 and $^{3}/_{12}$ or 24 years 3 months)

f. Is your design going to cause bias?

Would only a particular personality or belief respond honestly?

g. Is a personal interview or the filling out of a form more reliable?

2. Who are you going to survey?

The aim is to get a sample which covers the population in which you are interested. Are you going to limit the survey to teenagers? To whites or blacks? To upper middle class people? Is trying to cover the whole population range too ambitious, rendering the results meaningless? Will the survey be irrelevant if the whole population is not covered?

3. Given that there will be some bias in your sample, try to identify it and comment accordingly in your report.

4. How are you going to present the data?

The aim is to convey, as honestly as possible, the data to the reader. Is it best just to give them all the raw figures and let them analyze it themselves? Is some form of table or graph better to grasp the overview?

5. Are you going to provide an interpretation in words?

A summary of how you see the findings is usually the most interesting part. How are you going to present this?

Ideas for Statistical Analysis

1. Can we find tallies for various replies?

2. Can these results be best presented on a bar graph, pie graph, histogram, or table? Is statistical analysis unsuitable for your approach and, therefore, a discussion in essay or report form more appropriate?

3. Should we offer only a given number of answers to choose from, thus enabling a tally for each response?

   For example, *yes/no* or *sometimes/rarely/never,* or a compromise: *Christian/Jew/Moslem/other, please specify...*)

4. Would limiting the answers to those given mean that some people may find no answers that match their views?

5. Is this a reasonable trade-off to be able to come up with firm statistics?

6. Do some questions suit limited replies while others suit open-ended replies? For example, "What do you believe God looks like?"

7. Are there further statistical methods which could be applied to your data to draw out relevant features?

8. Is there a difference between the responses for females and males, young and old, and so on?

9. How could the results best be presented to convey their meaning?

10. Can you present the same results in two different ways which provide different conclusions? If so, prepare the two reports and test them on people to see if they do result in a different conclusion from the same results.

Thinking about Thinking

There is a big difference in emotional content in statistical analysis compared to discussions about beliefs.

Throughout this challenge you will keep a journal. Each entry will include how you feel about each stage. Is it easy or hard? Why?

Does the emotional sensitivity affect the level of difficulty?

Is it easier to tackle the problems of working out how to present statistics than it is to ask people about their religious beliefs?

Try to become conscious of how you feel about each stage of the task and how this affects the way in which you approach it.

At the end of the challenge, see what conclusions you can draw from the journal entries and how these can be applied to other aspects of your life. Are you sensitive to the feelings and rights to privacy of others?

Teacher's Notes

Cognitive Level

Bloom's Taxonomy

This assignment involves application of methods of collecting data, which is probably familiar to students, to a new situation. The emphasis is on the synthesis of a survey to complete a goal which is difficult by this method. It also involves a great deal of analysis.

Personal Characteristics

Gifted students often have an ability to work with abstract concepts, such as beliefs, which is beyond their age peers. They are also known to have a more developed interest in such concepts.

It is often reported that gifted children have a higher sense of morality and sensitivity to the feelings of others. They are also often very interested in emotional issues. This personality trait was the foremost consideration in designing this challenge.

Gifted children approach tasks in original and imaginative ways. Although this assignment has a fairly obvious route, it's designed so it can be adapted to allow such variation. This is not only in the ways in which the data are collected (can we trick people into revealing their beliefs by more subtle means than: What do you believe about God?) but in the reporting, interpretation, and reaction to the data collected.

General Notes

In discussing the results of the "Thinking about Thinking Journal," it is interesting to extrapolate the students' response to the stages of the assignment to their potential career options. The crucial contrast is that between working with an emotional content, such as in discussions about God, and the non-emotional task of statistical analysis.

The ability to handle a sensitive issue well is invaluable.

This assignment can be adapted to the individuals in the class. For example: A very able student mathematically should be encouraged to take the analysis to quite an advanced level. Standard techniques for the analysis of sociological data can be found in a number of references which cover statistics for the social sciences. The student could go as far as factor analysis, gaining valuable insights into the influences which affect our personal beliefs—such as gender, age, socioeconomic position, or religious background. The questions and format should reflect this approach to analysis.

A student whose interests are in the philosophical area should be encouraged to examine the data from this perspective. Such questions as the effect on society of a belief in God and the variety of interpretations of the concept would be relevant. Again, this student would need to design the survey to optimize this type of analysis.

A student who is interested in computers should be encouraged to use this interest in the production of the survey itself, the recording and analysis of the data, and the production of the report. This could include using the word processor, database, and/or spreadsheet for the same assignment—a valuable task.

A student who is interested in writing could use the data and ideas gained to write for publication in a magazine or newspaper. Alternatively, the student may wish to extrapolate from his or her data to write a fiction piece based on the interaction between people from the range of concepts in some situation which forces them to work together on something in which their concept of God was crucial.

A student who is interested in science may like to look at the relevance of these findings to the acceptance of evolution and any conflicts which may arise between what may be seen as disparate beliefs. Some people appear to be able to accept a firm belief in God and be competent scientists. Is their concept of God different from non-scientists? And so on.

It is important that this challenge can be manipulated to suit the students' own skills and talents; therefore, it is advised that you and your students negotiate the approach early in the assignment. Students may tend to take the approach which they think is correct and desired—a very common trait with gifted students—but should be encouraged to take risks and try to look at the assignment in their own personal way. This will introduce bias of course, but that must be seen in perspective. All answers from all approaches cannot be completed by a single person. A comparison at completion is valid.

A word of warning: some students are in doubt about their own beliefs. It is essential that no view is projected within the classroom as being right or more valid than another. It is this very issue, however, which makes very bright students interested in the nature of other people's beliefs and, more importantly, the reason they believe what they do.

It is also possible that a student may not wish to do this assignment. Although I have not encountered this problem, it is foreseeable. The reason may be due to background or embarrassment at asking people to reply to such questions. He or she may feel it is not a justified invasion of privacy. If so, it is possible to adjust the assignment to use historical figures whose beliefs are recorded.

Assessment

Criteria

To what level did the student:

1. analyze survey techniques as displayed in newspapers and magazines?

2. practice survey techniques using "safe" topics?

3. use a graduated set of survey topics to gain the necessary skills?

4. synthesize a survey format and technique for the question posed by the challenge?

5. consider methods which respected privacy while gaining the required information?

6. allow a person to graciously avoid answering the questions?

7. allow for the resulting bias in the analysis?

8. analyze the data?

9. present the data and analysis in a clear manner?

10. evaluate the validity of the findings of the survey?

Thinking about Thinking Report
In the report, to what level is the student able to analyze and evaluate:
11. her or his own feelings about each stage of the process?

12. the difficulties and why these aspects were difficult?

13. the effect of emotional sensitivity on the approach to the problem?
14. the difficulties associated with a clinical analysis such as the analysis of the collected data and the difficulties associated with asking people sensitive questions?

15. his or her own sensitivity to the feelings and right of privacy of others?

Challenge 12
The Future is Cool
(for Kold Korp.)

The Aim

1. To use skills gained in previous challenges and to develop skills to approach a large project containing many aspects. The skills include organization, division of responsibilities, considering limitations of scope due to time pressures, and producing a report presenting many aspects in a single format.

2. To let students follow a single theme in depth.

3. To force students to work on a contentious issue in a situation where their opinion on the issue is of no consequence.

Thinking about Thinking

To monitor thought processes over an extended assignment. To observe the conditions of mood, location, concentration, and intention at times of achievement.

In doing so, applying the ideas gained from monitoring thinking in the other challenges and trying to remain conscious of thinking skills/processes throughout the task.

Kold Korp.—Bid Specifications

Never being one to miss an opportunity, I have noticed a huge gap in the American market—we have no cryonics company. There are sure to be people who want to be frozen when they have nearly died from an incurable disease, to be revived when the technology allows them to be cured. Kold Korp. Ltd. is to be born!

There was the case of Roy Schiavello, America's first cryonics patient, who was declared clinically dead in 1990. The staff from the Australian company Alcor Life Extension Foundation then stepped in and Mr. Schiavello is now in Australia, at —130° Centigrade, waiting for a time when he can be restored to full life and a cure has been found for his brain tumor.

You will act as my consultant. You can work individually or as part of a team. I just need the information and guidance. I'll find the financing. I want to set up this business before anyone else does. I don't care what your opinion is on the morality of this venture or whether you'd like to be frozen.

What I want in your report is sections covering the following aspects in order for me to set up this business and make it successful. Your business, which will need an appropriate name, will offer a bid to Kold Korp. for the job of acting as my well-paid consultants in this project.

I will be interviewing all applicants on the date given. Please prepare a five to ten minute presentation to support your application. This may take any appropriate form and is intended to direct my attention to the salient features of your report.

In your written report I need as much information as possible before I can choose a consulting company. I am receiving bids from a number of companies.

Basic Scientific Background

The magazine <u>Discover</u> ran a special on this in November, 1987. Also try <u>New Scientist</u>, September 26, 1992, and other scientific journals, encyclopedias, newspaper files, people, and relevant "experts."

What I'll Need in Terms of Equipment

This should become clearer having looked at the technology involved. I need the equipment for the actual freezing and storage as well as that required for my office staff.

What I'll Need in Terms of Staff

Make sure you consider the fact that we will be running a business as well as a technology-based laboratory. We aim to attract clients and serve all aspects of their needs.

Survey Results of What Type of People Will Use My Services

I need this kind of information if I am to optimize my planning and advertising. Make sure a range of ages and backgrounds is included. I may wish to use a "subscribe in advance" method of financing.

Advertising Campaign

The above survey should help as a guide. I want an imaginative campaign, e.g. "Free measure and quote."

Some Idea of the Financial Requirements

There are sure to be some accountants or business studies experts who will help you. Note: My aim is to make a profit. I am not in this business to provide a service out of a moral obligation to humankind.

Psychological Needs (We Care!)

Assuming the client will be frozen for 100 years, consider the changes over the last 100 years and what could change in the next 100 years. Also, what do people need for emotional well-being? From these considerations, advise me on the strategies I should use when my client signs up and when he or she comes back. Although I am basically interested in building a successful business, I do want to care for my clients.

You may get some ideas by looking at some of Oliver Sacks' work in the book and film "Awakenings." The film "Ice Man" may also give some ideas of the problems of waking up in a world which is unfamiliar—technologically, educationally, socially, and in terms of belief systems.

Legal Considerations

Find a friendly lawyer, legal studies teacher or any other expert to point you in the right direction. Frankly, I doubt anyone will use our services without some kind of contract.

Concerns Expressed in the Community

There are many people who will not be impressed with this kind of business. I need to be aware of their concerns to be prepared for protests. I expect these to be based on religious grounds. Am I right or wrong in that assumption? I have also been attacked by a conservationist who pointed out that if everybody did this, and "death were no more," we would have a massive overpopulation problem. I have been asked to go before a Senate Committee to discuss some kind of legislation controlling the market in cryonics. Should the only prerequisite be the ability to pay? They have been asked to make recommendations to the government. Please advise me.

Any Other Aspects Which You Perceive as Relevant
Please note that I have asked a number of companies to present a report outlining their abilities to act as my advisors. The company whose report is the most comprehensive will be hired to act as my consultants for the next few years.

I look forward to your report and my future business success.

(Ms) C. U. Laeta

Thinking about Thinking
You are to be yourself as well as the character you take on as part of this assignment. As yourself, you will monitor your thoughts.

Consider such questions as:

What triggered this idea?

What were you able to achieve at the time?

What was your mood at the time?

Were you concentrating on the assignment or doing something else?

Where were you located at the time?

Did someone or something else contribute to conceiving the idea or achieving the result?

Is there a different process involved when coming up with ideas to completing a section of the report?

Is there a difference between working on the advertising campaign and devising the legal contract?

Did some aspects worry you more than others? If so, which did you start with or choose to tackle, and why?

If you worked in a group, how did this affect your thinking, behavior, and working style?

Did the personal opinions or experiences of yourself or anyone else affect the way in which you approached the task? If so, how and why? Is it possible to avoid such biases or are they of benefit?

What was the motivation at crucial times in the process? Were you interested in the assignment, hoping to please or impress someone, aiming for a high assessment, pushing yourself for personal satisfaction, just trying to get it done because you'd left everything to the last minute, again?

Are there any other features you were aware of as you worked on the various aspects of this assignment? Any observations you have may be relevant. Note them all down to sift through when the assignment is finished.

And most importantly:
How can I best use my thinking skills?

Self-evaluation Sheet
1. Write a summary of how you went about the challenge

    a. as an individual.

    b. as part of a group (if you did).

2. List the things in your presentation which you thought were good. Why did you think they were good?

3. List the things in your presentation which you thought could have been improved. In what way could they have been improved and what was the disappointing aspect?

4. List the things in your report which you thought were good. Why did you think they were good?

5. List the things in your report which you thought could have been improved. In what way could they have been improved and what was the disappointing aspect?

6. If you were given the same task again, in what ways would you approach it differently? Why?

7. What is your view of the role of cryonics in our society? Do you think a company such as Kold Korp. could be successfully established? Should it be?

8. **Thinking about Thinking**

   If possible, compare notes with other students about the way you approached the task and completed it.

"He's not dead yet - there's a chance he might get better."

Were there any patterns? Maybe there were times or places which were more productive. Many people get all their best ideas in the shower. Did you make any such observations? Einstein claimed he produced his best results by combining intense concentration with musing while on walks. Did you combine a variety of approaches to produce the aspects of the assignments with which you were most happy?

If you can identify patterns or ways of enhancing the quality of your work, you can optimize your processes in all of life's big assignments!

Teacher's Notes

Cognitive Level

Bloom's Taxonomy
This is a flexible assignment which can be used to emphasize various levels of the taxonomy. It is especially valid for comprehension, application, and synthesis.

It can also be used to examine the role of evaluation. If moral judgments are made before the topic has been examined thoroughly, the students' ability to work with an issue is reduced. Far too often students are asked to argue for one side or another of a controversial issue. Having chosen their "side," they research the issue. One of the aims in designing this challenge was to take a highly controversial issue and develop a major assignment in which the students' view on the issue was irrelevant. It is worthwhile, however, to complete the assignment with a discussion of the personal views of the student once he or she has completed the work.

Personal Characteristics

It is rewarding for very bright students to delve into a topic in depth. This is rarely done in a way which crosses the boundaries of the disciplines. Such a challenge involves the need to use resources and present a report involving scientific, legal, financial, artistic, social, and communication areas.

One of the often-quoted characteristics of gifted children is their desire to collect information. They also have a heightened awareness of aspects of life which involve emotional issues. This assignment responds to these characteristics.

General Notes

This is a very involved assignment which can go on indefinitely; therefore, a time limit should be set. It can be run with groups or individuals. I have had both working in a classroom. Groups can set up companies and delegate responsibilities. They will learn about teamwork and the role of an individual in a team situation. I have found the assignment works well if carried out over a holiday break as this allows students to receive replies from the businesses or experts they have contacted.

Some of the best assignments have been produced by students working alone.

One student advised me to abandon my aims for cryonics and concentrate on research to master the use of "Thyroidics" based on the medical condition described in "Awakenings." He supported his advice with scientific and financial arguments.

I pointed out to groups which had formed in the classroom that all groups were single sex and questioned the wisdom of this. One boy who was working alone approached one of the brightest girls who had been chosen as managing director of her company and asked her to join his company as his secretary. I am pleased to report that her response was, "Get real!"

The assignment allows for a range of talents to be used, as well as the introduction of humor. I have had some excellent company names from "Frozen Assets" to "Chill Factor." The advertising campaigns have proved most imaginative. Students who like to tackle the difficult tasks have gone to great lengths with the legal and financial aspects of the assignment. I have also had business cards drawn up and cases of industrial espionage. This is not an assignment with a predictable outcome.

This work also lets students look at company structures and the role of consultants. Using their imaginations, many are able to create very interesting companies.

I have also had a student who felt unable to work on this task which she found morally unacceptable. Her excellent report detailed her objections to accepting a consulting position when she felt the product was not valid. This led to a great class discussion on the position of an advertising employee whose company accepts a contract for a product which the employee feels unable to praise. It also led us into the concept of a legal firm accepting a contract to defend someone whom they felt was guilty.

The local office of a large life insurance company had trouble responding to my student's phone call on the status of the frozen person in terms of their pay-out. The initial response was silence and then a promise to call back. Eventually a senior member of the company called from headquarters stating that the company would rely on the legal definitions of death. We were thanked for raising an issue which the company had not considered.

A student has now collected evidence, for which he claims a strong scientific basis, showing that upon revival the person would have limited memory, if any. Does this make the entire process irrelevant?

The point of these anecdotal notes is to show the numerous ways in which this assignment can be tackled depending on the emphasis chosen.

In the analysis of the "Thinking about Thinking" section, it is worth discussing the findings so that students can identify the ways in which they can maximize their creative thought processes. It may be that taking a walk midway through a task optimizes the flow of original ideas. (Einstein found it valuable!) It may be that students discover aspects of such an assignment which require analysis of scientific, legal, or financial information are better done at a desk in a quiet situation. They may find that group work stimulates great ideas for advertising, but the accounts are better drawn up by an individual who is able to concentrate without interruption.

Such variations make for valuable discussion. It is also important to discuss how these ideas can be applied in other areas of study and life.

Criteria

Assessment

To what level did the student analyze and present:
1. the scientific background?

2. the equipment needs?

3. the staffing needs?

4. the survey results?

5. the necessary advertising campaign?

6. the financial requirements?

7. the psychological needs?

8. the legal considerations?

9. the concerns expressed in the community?

To what level did the student:

10. creatively present the company's report?

11. role play the consultant's part?

12. evaluate the report?

13. evaluate the presentation?

14. justify his or her personal view of the role of cryonics?

Thinking about Thinking Report

In the report, to what level is the student able to analyze and evaluate:

15. the times, situations, and moods associated with the occurrence of ideas?

16. the various thought processes associated with working on different stages of the report?

17. the way in which the assignment was approached in terms of the many different aspects to be considered?

18. the motivational aspects involved in tackling the problem?

19. the patterns which may have occurred in thinking while completing such a long-term assignment?

20. ways which might optimize his or her use of thinking skills in other long-term assignments in life?

Challenges 13 and 14
Single-Task Thinking

Most of the thinking we are obliged to do does not require total concentration. We can think about other things at the same time. To use computer parlance, we can multi-task. We can cook, listen to the radio, and hold a conversation simultaneously—and still not be taxing our minds at all.

But for these challenges I am interested in tasks which require more than normal levels of concentration—tasks which force our minds to the level of thinking which blocks out all other stimuli.

Single-task thinking is used when a level of concentration is required beyond that which can be naturally performed without deliberate effort. It is required to solve puzzles in which many parts of logic are required simultaneously, all needing to be retained within the conscious thought level.

It happens during a particularly complicated game of chess. It happens when you solve a puzzle such as the Rubix cube (before the solution book becomes available). It happens when you have to get the school timetable right—keeping all variables in mind. I suspect for most people it never happens. Few people can be bothered solving such puzzles. Few people can be bothered running a marathon. The latter isn't for everyone. Neither is single-task thinking. But it is for intellectually gifted students.

There is much evidence that the great creative thinkers, such as Einstein, worked at intense levels interspersed with times of deliberate non-control or musing. It appears that the combination may be of optimum value in problem solving exercises.

Gifted children may be able to cope with virtually all tasks set within the normal curriculum without ever being required to force themselves into the single-task level. In discussions with older students I have found that many are conscious of this higher level of concentration and are surprised to find others also thinking this way. They have never been asked to be aware of exactly what their minds are doing.

My father was a pioneer in the computer industry. He talked of blanking his mind deliberately when the complexities of the logic of the computer program he was developing were beyond that of which he felt capable. He would often gain the logic plan and go back over the steps to show that his solution was correct. In those days computer programs were all in assembly language with no library routines as are available with the languages we use now. Every memory location in the CPU and every operation the computer made had to be in the programmer's memory concurrently.

He was making his mind do something which "he" was not capable of doing normally.

When discussing this form of thinking with students, many seem familiar with the state, but find it difficult to express the feeling of total concentration to the exclusion of all other mental activity. Most express it in terms of the feeling when the stream of logic is interrupted and they are left with no idea of the path which led them to the present step and, therefore, have to start again.

I have now used the term "single-task" thinking to express this level. As with similar computer terms, I happily use the term as both an adjective and a verb. It is beyond just concentrating. It is total absorption and a forcing of the brain to work at maximum potential in a very narrow focus. I am sure there is a time limit, as with all activities which exercise a muscle to its extremes. Maybe this time limit can be extended with practice and thus increased "fitness."

In completing these challenges I hope students will start to become conscious of the depths of concentration which are required and can, therefore, learn to move into this single-task state. I am convinced that it can be called upon and controlled with practice—as many students do during logically difficult exams. A very bright student completing assignments which are entirely at the knowledge and comprehension levels of the Bloom's taxonomy can spend his or her entire school days multitasking—math and what's going on outside the window and last night's TV and tonight's basketball game and the teacher's strange hairstyle all mulling around together.

By asking students to do something more than just learn and understand someone else's knowledge, I hope to move them towards controlling and using single-task levels of thinking. Hence, making students conscious of their thought processes as well as their thought content is a most valuable exercise.

This aspect is explored in the following two challenges.

Challenge 13
If Fred's Hat Is Purple,
What's the Name of Mary's Dog?

1. To practice single-task thinking by completing logic puzzles.
2. To become systematic in the design and testing of simple logic puzzles.
3. To become conscious of thinking levels and the number of tasks being conducted at once.

The Aim

Consider the following puzzles:

Method

1. Three little girls loved three little boys. The three little boys loved them in return. (Isn't this delightful?) Alan and Christopher and Billy love Mimmy and Nanny and Liz.

   But the rotten little gossipmongers in the playground spread the following rotten rumors:

   > Alan loves Mimmy.
   > Mimmy loves Billy.
   > Billy loves Liz.

Like all good rumors, none was true. All the little romances were blissfully happy. (This is so sweet!)

Who really loves dear little Liz?

2. There are four extremely talented students in this class. Each of them plays a musical instrument to perfection—and none of them the same instrument as any other. They each are experts in their own right on a particular novelist—and each of them has their own writer with whom he or she is enraptured.

> Margaret plays the cello.
> The violinist is an expert on Tolstoy.
> Vincent is not an oboist.
> The student who knows all about DuMaurier is not Lionel.
> Margaret has never read Ibsen.
> Rebecca doesn't play the violin and has no interest in Shakespeare.
> Vincent is not fond of Tolstoy.
> Lionel doesn't play the harp.
> The oboist can't stand Ibsen.

So who is Rebecca's writer, and with which instrument does she sing his or her praises?

3. There are five trainers at Poochies' Training College: Poddy Poodle, Terry Terrier, Sandy Spaniel, Darren "Tiny" Dane and Marsha Mongrel. Each of these train two of the ten resident dogs. There are two poodles, two terriers, two spaniels, two great danes, and two mongrels.

> Each trainer trains two different breeds of dog.
> None of them trains his or her own name-sake.
> The name-sakes of the two dogs trained by Tiny train terriers.
> The name-sakes of the dogs which Marsha trains both train poodles.
> Poddy Poodle trains a spaniel and a terrier.

What dogs does Sandy Spaniel train?

4. Having completed the three puzzles, it is clear the sort of problem I'm proposing. They can be hard or simple, interesting or dull. I want them to be interesting. They should range from simple to hard. Make up five each. Be careful, it is essential they have only one solution.

5. As you worked on these puzzles, did you become aware of times when you needed to concentrate deeply to keep the variables in your

head while you eliminated possibilities? Describe the various levels of thinking in your own words.

6. If you are working in a group, share the puzzles with others, testing them on each other. First, test that the solutions are unique. Second, have the other students rate your puzzles as simple, medium, or difficult.

   Can you come up with some guidelines to making up puzzles so they have a unique solution?
   Can you come up with some guidelines as to how to vary the difficulty?

7. Having completed your five puzzles and rated them, try them on people outside the group. Have you, and others working on this assignment, improved your ability to complete this sort of puzzle? If so, this is the reason you must test them on non-experienced puzzlers.

8. Monitor your thinking for one day. Take a note-pad with you and make brief notes about the levels of concentration required for various tasks. What proportion of the day required concentration on one task alone? At some times of the day were you aware of your brain coping with many conscious tasks at once? (Mother, TV, homework, and rumbling stomach?)

   Do not include autonomic tasks such as breathing.
   Does your mind refuse to concentrate on some tasks and drift off of its own accord? When, why, and what to?

9. Write a report covering the following points:

   a. The five puzzles.

   b. The results of the trials.

   c. Your analysis of the results of the trials. Were your predictions accurate? Did anyone come up with an alternative solution?

   d. Your personal description of the way you think when creating puzzles. Were you aware of parts of this task which could be done with your brain at half pace? Some sections which required reasonable concentration? Some sections which required forced, intense concentration? Can you describe these processes and what determined each?

e. Can you control your level of concentration? How? Why would you want to? Are there any other observations you can make on your thinking processes over the course of this task?

f. Your observations on monitoring your thinking. Did monitoring the situation get in the way? Well, it is another task!

Teacher's Notes

Bloom's Taxonomy

There is a degree of comprehension involved. Application of methods for solution and creation of puzzles is used. The emphasis is on analysis. The synthesis involves creating new puzzles using the ideas gained from the analysis of other examples. There is also the synthesis and analysis of the testing procedures. Some evaluation of the puzzles is done, but this is fairly straightforward.

Cognitive Level

Solving abstract puzzles is a love of most intelligent children. It is rare that they are given the opportunity to create and test them. Gifted students often have an interest in the abstract, and examining their own thinking is pretty abstract!

Personal Characteristics

Intellectually able students are those who have mental talents. To optimize use of them they should become familiar with the workings of the tool they depend upon—their mind. It is not the physiological but the mental processing with which they need to become comfortable in order to use it to the best of their abilities.

General Notes

It's valuable to monitor what the mind is doing during any given task. I am convinced we could produce more able students if we gave them time to monitor the thought processes which they use.

The main problem with this task is testing the puzzles on other students if the puzzles do not have a unique solution, i.e. they are overspecified or they do not have a solution at all.

There are many examples in puzzle books if you want more for students to analyze first.

It is also possible to repeat the task using other standard forms of puzzles. The task can be varied to use mathematical puzzles for the mathematically able and word puzzles for the linguistic stars. This extension can go on in many forms, depending on the interest of the students. I have run competitions for puzzle generation which have been very successful.

Challenging Minds

It is interesting how imaginative the scenarios can become.

"Jenny knew she'd find reason here somewhere."

Students are often very proud of their puzzles. They can be typed up, once tested, into a booklet and reproduced for distribution in or out of class. Students do come up with puzzles as good as those which are commercially available, although some have been mind-bogglingly hard!

Answers to the puzzles:
1. Alan loves Liz.
   Christopher and Minny are practically engaged.
   Bill and Nanny.

2. Rebecca plays the oboe magnificently and dotes on DuMaurier.
   Vincent plays the harp and adores Ibsen.
   Lionel plays violin while, at the same time, reading Tolstoy.
   Margaret plays cello and lives for reading Shakespeare.

3. Sandy Spaniel trains a mongrel and a great dane.
   Poddy has a spaniel and a terrier.
   Marsha rules a terrier and a great dane.
   Tiny deals with a poodle and a mongrel.
   Terry was eaten by a poodle and a spaniel.

Criteria

To what level did the student:

1. set five puzzles with unique solutions?

Assessment 2. present puzzles with interesting and varied scenarios?

3. produce a set of guidelines for constructing such puzzles?

4. analyze the way in which varying degrees of difficulty can be introduced into the puzzles?

5. rate the puzzles?

6. test the puzzles?

7. evaluate the puzzles produced?

Thinking about Thinking Report
In the report, to what level is the student able to analyze and evaluate:
 8. the various levels of thinking required for this assignment?

 9. the various levels of thinking required over a day?

10. the external influences on the levels of concentration?

11. her ability to control her levels of concentration?

12. the effect of monitoring his thinking on his thinking process?

Challenge 14
Please Ignore This Heading

A Paradoxical Challenge

Did you obey the heading?

The Aim

1. To develop the skill of concentrating to maximum depth on a single task.

2. To understand and improve levels of concentration.

There is much evidence to show that the most productive and creative people work at two levels of thinking as discussed in the section headed "Single-task Thinking." The ability to control and use deep levels of concentration can lead to an ability to solve problems beyond the level of 'normal' capability. This exercise is designed to investigate these ideas.

Method

1. Take the first two paradoxes (numbered 1 and 2, including the heading) and explain, in writing, why it is a paradox and the consequence of accepting its truth.

   Do so under a strict time limit, e.g. 10 minutes.

   Explain the paradoxes in clear English and have someone read your explanation to see if it makes sense.

2. Describe your thought processes, any interruptions, what happened if you were interrupted, and so on. Do so in writing.

3. Repeat the process with Paradox 3. Again, describe your thinking. You have 10 minutes.

4. Repeat the process for Paradox 4, be conscious of both your process and your explanation.

   Does this make it impossible?

5. Choose five more paradoxes from the list and repeat the process in 30 minutes. Is there a time limit or fatigue process involved? Are there optimum times for intense concentration? Is 10 minutes intense, five minutes off, 10 minutes intense more productive than 25 minutes of continuous concentrating?

6. Without writing down the explanations, try to explain to yourself five more of the paradoxes. Does the process of writing help or hinder you? Is there some optimum method?

7. Using all of the paradoxes, try to improve your ability to work at a deeper level. Group the paradoxes according to difficulty in explaining. Choose the five most difficult paradoxes and try to come up with clear explanations. Are you becoming conscious of various levels of concentration? Can you describe ways in which you can control your skills?

Paradoxes

1. See heading on page 124.

2. The Megarian Paradox or Liar Paradox or Eubilides Paradox:

   A man says, "I am lying." Is he?

3. The Paradox of Protagoras:

   The lawyer from the 5th century B.C., Protagoras, asked his pupil to pay for his instruction when he had won his first case. But no clients appeared. So Protagoras said, "I will sue you for the money. If I win you pay me. If you win, you pay me as per our agreement."

   "Nay," said his pupil, "if I win then the court rules I need not pay you, but if you win, I still haven't won, so I don't pay."

4. Zeno's tale of Achilles and the tortoise:

   Achilles, the great runner, is to race the tortoise. To make the race fairer, the tortoise is allowed to start. When Achilles starts, the tortoise has already reached Point 1. To pass the tortoise Achilles must first reach Point 1. Meanwhile the tortoise has moved onto Point 2. To pass the tortoise, Achilles then has to reach Point 2. Meanwhile the tortoise has moved onto Point 3. To pass the tortoise, Achilles has to reach Point 3. Meanwhile the tortoise ...

So Achilles can never beat the tortoise.

But what if Achilles aimed for a future position of the tortoise, could he beat him there?

5. All generalizations are false.

6. I know that no knowledge is possible.

7. There are no absolutes.

8. There is nothing which is certain.

9. There is nothing which exists.

10. I do not exist.

11. All rules have exceptions.

12. Never say "never."

13. The more you know, the more you know you don't know.

14. The exception proves the rule.

15. What happens when an irresistible force meets an immovable object?

16. Just trust me when I tell you that you should never trust a man who says "trust me."

17. To endure the unendurable is true endurance.
　　　　　　　　　　　　　　　　　—Japanese proverb

18. He lifted himself up by his own bootstraps.

19. Please answer the next question with a "yes" or "no."
Will you answer "no"?

20. The Paradox of God's omnipotence.

If God is all-powerful:

a. Can he create a circle which is a square?

b. Can he change the past?

c. Can he move an object which is to him immovable?

d. Can he create a problem which is to him insolvable?

e. Can he destroy himself such that he is unable to return to life?

f. Can he deny his own existence?

g. (Pascal's version) God is not all-powerful as he cannot build a wall he cannot jump.

21. Socrates: What Plato is about to say is false.
    Plato: Socrates has just spoken truly.

22. P. E. B. Jourdain's Cards:

Jourdain produced a card with one statement on each side. The statements were:

The statement on the other side of this card is false.
The statement on the other side of this card is true.

23. The Clock Paradox has been argued for 50 years since Albert Einstein's theory of relativity predicted that clocks would run more slowly when read by an observer moving relative to the clock, than when read by someone in the same frame of reference as the clock. This defied all concepts of time as the ultimate constant. This was argued in the terms of the "Twin Paradox" in which one twin is imagined to leave the earth in a rocketship at high speed while the other

stays on earth. In this case, when the rocketing twin returns to earth he will be younger, (will have aged less having had less of his minutes pass) than his twin at home. Are they still twins?

This paradoxical situation has been experimentally supported. If you wish to follow it up, try Carl Sagan's excellent book *Cosmos* or watch the television film called "Einstein's Universe" with Peter Ustanov.

24. Supertasks:

Philosophers, recently, have been discussing a paradox of infinity, called supertasks. They use a Thompson lamp. The lamp is turned on and off by a push-button switch. It is turned on for half a minute, then off for a quarter of a minute, then on for an eighth of a minute, then off for a sixteenth of a minute, and so on.

As the sum of the series:

$$1/2 + 1/4 + 1/8 + 1/16 + 1/32 + 1/64 + \ldots = 1$$

is the lamp on or off at the end of one minute?

25. The Hedonistic paradox:

If a person goes forth in the constant search for pleasure for himself, he will not find it. If, however, he spends his time seeking pleasure for others, he will, himself, be the recipient of pleasure.

26. Bertrand Russell proposed the paradox of the barber of Seville:

"A man of Seville is shaved by the Barber of Seville if and only if the man does not shave himself. Does the Barber of Seville shave himself?"

27. The Author's poetry:

Line 2 of this poem, I can vouch is true.
Line 3, without doubt, can be trusted by you.
Line 4 is one on which you can rely,
but line 1 is most definitely a lie.

28. The question of Seng-Ts'an:

If you work on your mind, with your mind, how can you avoid immense confusion?

29. Grelling, a German mathematician, in 1908 proposed the paradox of heterology:

Adjectives can be divided into 2 types:
1. those which refer to themselves, e.g. ENGLISH and SHORT.
2. those which do not refer to themselves, such as LONG and GERMAN.

Type 1 are called autological. Type 2 are called heterological.

Is the adjective "heterological" itself heterological?

30. "There is nothing so unthinkable as thought unless it is the entire absence of thought."

—Samuel Butler

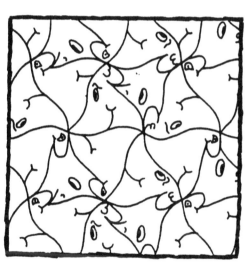

31. The paradox of the meeting agenda:

I object to any meeting which is not run formally. In order to put any motion it is essential that a motion has been passed which allows the motion to be put.

32. The teacher's friend:

Stand in the corner and do not come out until you can guarantee to me that you are not thinking about a pure white wombat.

33. Believing:

I believe people only believe what they want to—but I wish they didn't.

34. Instantaneous Movement:

At any given instant, a moving car is stationary. If time is but a continuum of instances, how can a car ever move? It must, at all time, be stationary.

35. Proof: 1 = 2

Let a = b	a = b
Multiply both sides by a	$a^2 = ab$
Subtract b from both sides	$a^2 - b^2 = ab - b^2$
Factor	(a-b)(a+b) = b(a-b)
Canceling the (a-b) brackets	a + b = b
But, a = b, so	b + b = b
So	2b = b
so	2 = 1
	QED

36. Towers:

We need an eight-centimeter high tower. Eight centimeters is a finite height. Blocks are very solid things. This, however, is a very strange tower. The first block is four centimeters thick. The next is half that—two centimeters. The next is half again—just one centimeter. The next, just half a centimeter, and so on. How many blocks are there in this tower?

Why is there a problem? I could start with an eight-centimeter high tower, and cut it to make the blocks, couldn't I? I cut it in half, and place one block on the floor. Then I cut the remaining block and put one on top of the first, and so on. Easy!

It is only the limitations of my woodworking tools that cause me to fail. With perfect tools, I could construct this tower! Or could I?

37. Bertrand Russell proposed the famous paradox of Tristam Shandy:

"Tristam Shandy, as we know, took two years writing the history of the first two days of his life, and lamented that, at this rate, material would accumulate faster than he could deal with it, so that he could never come to an end. Now, I maintain that if he had lived forever, and not wearied of his task, then, even if his life had continued as eventfully as it began, no part of his biography would have remained unwritten."

38. "The superfluous, a very necessary thing."
                                              – Voltaire

39. A version of the Prediction Paradox:

"You have to go to the dentist at some stage this year, my dear," said the adoring mother.
"So you won't lose sleep the night before worrying about it, I promise I will never let you lose a night's sleep by knowing the appointment is the following day."
"Great," said the cavitous child, "then I'll never have to go! See, if it was the last day of the year, I'd know the night before, because there'd be no other days left. So it can't be the last day of the year.
"So it can't be the second last day, because I know it can't be the last day, so I'd know the night before the second last day if it was to be that day, so it can't be the second last day.
"And it can't be the third last day, because I know it can't be the second last day..."

40. A "Complete History of the World to Now" must include the "Complete History of the World to Now"—completed—or it will not be complete.

41. M.C. Escher's artwork, especially his later impossibilities, are examples of visual paradoxes. If you have not yet become familiar with them, do yourself a good turn and study them.

(see Challenge 10—"Dare to be Different: A Hypothesis")

Part 2
It may interest some students to take this further into the area of classification. Classifying paradoxes will rival classifying humor in difficulty. It has been argued for many years by some of the world's greatest thinkers—so you're in good company.

Classification

Now, here are some definitions which are to help you begin classifying the above paradoxes. These are just a starting point; there are many more available in reference books.

Paradox (as defined by the *Dictionary of Philosophy*) is:

"Paradox (Greek, *paradoxon* from para 'contrary to' and doxa 'opinion').

1. A statement (tenet, belief, concept, notion) which is contrary to accepted opinion, or opposed to what is regarded as common sense, but which may be true.

2. A statement which on the surface appears absurd or even self-contradictory, but which is true or may be true.

3. An apparent dichotomy (or self-contradiction) which, when overcome, denies something that is regarded as true.

4. A situation where two statements that are incongruent (contrary, exclusive of each other) both appear to be true, and both must be accepted in action.

5. A statement which, when regarded as true, leads to its being false, and which, when regarded as false, leads to its truth (or leads to a truth)."

Peter A. Angeles goes on to define a logical paradox:

> "Paradox, logical: In general, a logical paradox is composed of two contrary, or contradictory, statements, both of which seem to have good supporting arguments. Compare with antinomy. A logical paradox results when two acceptable lines of argument lead to conclusions that seem contrary or contradictory. Logical paradoxes may be the consequence of:
>
> 1. a misapplication of the rules of logic;
>
> 2. a violation of the rules of logic which cannot be clearly expressed (or is not clearly seen); or

3. the inapplicability of the rules of logic to the situation. Some reformation of the logic is necessary either to avoid the paradox or to resolve it."

By the way, he defines *antinomy* as:

"Antimony (Greek, antithesis, from anti, "against," and nomos, "law"). A contradiction between two principles, each of which appears to be true but which cannot both be true. Often regarded as an extreme kind of paradox."

In the *Fontana Dictionary of Modern Thought* edited by Alan Bullock, Oliver Stallybrass and Stephen Trombley, paradox is defined as:

"Paradox: A statement which appears acceptable but which has unacceptable or contradictory consequences. Three kinds of paradoxes have proved important in the development of logic and mathematics.

1. Paradoxes of the infinite. Zeno of Elea argued thus: space is infinitely divisible; so an arrow must pass through infinitely many points in its flight; therefore, it can never reach the target. This (like many variants) is resolved by the theory of convergence to a limit: an infinite sequence can have a finite limit.

2. Semantic paradoxes. Epimenides the Cretan said (and was believed by Saint Paul):
"The Cretans are always liars." If true, the statement would have made the speaker an invariable liar, and would, therefore, have been false. Therefore, it must be false. (For another example see *heterological*.)

3. Paradoxes of set theory. Bertrand Russell considered the class (or set) R which consists of just those classes that do not belong to themselves. The R belongs to itself if, and only if, it does not."

The fascinating book *Vicious Circles and Infinity—An Anthology of Paradoxes* by Patrick Hughes and George Brecht suggests dividing logical paradoxes into *self-reference, contradiction,* and *vicious circle.*

1. Self-reference: a statement which becomes a paradox as it refers to itself.

   One form is the infinite regress: likened to a pair of mirrors facing one another, where the refection in one is then reflected back into the other which is then reflected back into the other which is then reflected back into the other which is then reflected back into the other which is ...

   Or the book, which has on its cover, a photo of someone reading the self-same book, which has on its cover a photo of someone the self-same book, which has on its cover ... OK?

2. A paradox which is a contradiction causes some logical conclusion which disagrees with the original statement.

   A circular contradiction is two or more statements which, when linked, form an impossible set of statements because they force other statements to be untrue when claimed as true.

3. Vicious circle: go round in a circle, but do not go round and round, e.g. Please Ignore This Heading.

There are many more definitions and classifications of paradoxes to be found in a large range of references. If you're after more—find a library and ask.

Teacher's Notes

Bloom's Taxonomy

This assignment would be heavily into the analysis level of the taxonomy. This is not just due to the analysis of the paradoxes, but also in the analysis of thinking processes. It is also asking for a synthesis of a theory about the way in which students can maximize their own concentration process. This is getting into a very abstract area for students, but should be a valuable skill for approaching all mentally demanding tasks in the future.

Cognitive Level

Gifted children are known for their ability to handle higher levels of abstraction. They are also noted for an intellectual curiosity and an ability to see complex relationships.

Paradoxes seem to fascinate very bright students. The ability to enjoy the intellectual challenge will be extended by the requirement to express complex ideas clearly.

Personal Characteristics

Before you have students screaming at you about number 35, let me tell you the error. The line which "cancels" the (a-b) brackets is in fact dividing through by (a-b). As the original assumption was that a=b, this is in fact dividing through by 0—hence the problem.

> Is this an error or a paradox?
> I think it is just plain incorrect mathematics!

General Notes

There are some examples which may or may not be considered as true paradoxes, depending on the definition used. I have tried to give a broad range to allow as much material for discussion as possible.

There are many more paradoxes waiting to be discovered by your students. The delight in sharing a newly discovered paradox with others is well known. It may be worth starting some kind of scrap book for the group.

I would like to emphasize the value of taking time to think about the way we think. It is rarely done, yet can be one of the most valuable exercises in optimizing the use of our reasoning capacities.

Challenging Minds

Assessment

Criteria
To what level did the student:
1. explain the first two paradoxes in clear English?

2. have his or her explanations assessed by others?

3. explain Paradoxes 3 and 4?

4. explain 5 paradoxes of choice?

5. (if Part 2 was done) construct a classification for paradoxes?

Thinking about Thinking Report
In the report, to what level is the student able to analyze and evaluate:
6. the thought processes involved?

7. the effect of interruptions on concentration?

8. his or her ability to be conscious of both the monitoring of the thinking and the process of explaining paradoxes at the same time?

9. the effect of mental fatigue?

10. the possibility of time limits on concentration?

11. the effect of writing explanations on the ability to explain a paradox?

12. his or her consciousness of various levels of concentration?

13. his or her ability to control concentration?

CPSIA information can be obtained
at www.ICGtesting.com
Printed in the USA
LVHW060146151020
668872LV00010B/161

9 781882 664207